Technique and Skill Drills

of the
World's Top Teams and Coaches

Edited by
Mike Saif

Published by
WORLD CLASS COACHING

First published April, 2002 by
WORLD CLASS COACHING 9205 W. 131 Terr, Overland Park, KS 66213 (913) 402-0030

ISBN 0-9718218-3-6

Edited by Mike Saif

WORLD CLASS COACHING would like to thank worldofsoccer.com for the use of the graphics

Published by

WORLD CLASS COACHING

Table of Contents

Alan Irvine 5

Alan Irvine 6

U.S. Women's World Cup Team 9

D.C. United 11

F.C. Petrolul Ploiesti, Romania 13

Mike Smith 15

Dallas Burn 18

PSV Eindhoven 20

FK Teplice U15 Youth Team 22

FK Teplice U17 Youth Team 26

Sammy Lee 29

Chicago Fire 32

D.C. United 33

Coaching Young Players 35

Ajax F.C. 40

Liverpool F.C. 41

Liverpool U17's & U19's 42

Nepal National Team 44

Barnsley F.C. 46

L.A. Galaxy 49

Coaching Young Players 51

Leeds United U17 Youth Team 54

Coaching Young Players 56

Humber College 59

Ajax U17 Youth Team 60

Chicago Fire 63

Coaching Young Players 64

Mick Hennigan 65

PSV Eindhoven Youth Team 67

Technique and Skill Drills

of the
World's Top Teams and Coaches

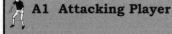 A1 Attacking Player	Path of Player	Path of Dribble	
D1 Defending Player	Path of Ball	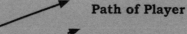 Target Area	

Interview With Alan Irvine

In January 1999 I spent the day with Alan Irvine, youth team coach at Newcastle United. Below is an interview where Irvine shares his thoughts on developing young players.

What do you think are the key aspects of a successful team?
Obviously you need very good players if you are to have a successful team. I also believe you need to have intelligent players. I think we need to get away from the style of coaching that doesn't allow the players to make decisions for themselves. We need players that can make decisions based on how the game is going, what the opposition is doing, etc.

How do you get that message across to your players?
I think part of my job is to make sure the players understand all the different options available to them and not to tell them which option they should choose for a particular circumstance. So, a good player will be one that makes more of the right decisions during a game.

What is your ideal playing formation?
It really depends on the players. I was a winger and I love to play with wingers, so something like a 4-3-3 with two wingers and a central striker with midfielders pushing up would be ideal. However, we don't have wingers in our team right now so I can't play that formation. I also believe it is wrong to play young players (16 to 19 years old) out of position too much just so you can play a certain formation. These young players are all hoping to sign professional contracts and they need to be given every chance possible to show what they are capable of in their favorite position.

Do you play with a sweeper and markers or a flat back four defense?
I have never played with a sweeper and two markers. However, I would consider playing with a sweeper in the same way the Germans do. Although, a 16 to 19-year-old sweeper wouldn't be very experienced and could end up being a defender that stays at the back and doesn't get much chance to tackle, head the ball or be involved much in the game. Our younger age groups play the same way. Sweepers are rarely used, and if so, they are given the freedom to play similar to the German style and look for opportunities to push up and join in the attacking possessions.

As the Director of the Youth Academy at Newcastle United, what are your responsibilities?
I am responsible for the players' development from U9's up to the full-time youth players age U16 - U19.

What kind of training sessions are done with the younger players age U9 - U12?
With the 9-year olds we work on technique. I believe the tactical side of things is not that important at that age. More important is, can they handle the ball? Are they able to pass, receive, turn and dribble the ball and be comfortable and confident doing it? Also, we don't do any work on defending mainly because defending is easier than being creative with the ball. Also, at that early age, there isn't that much to defend because in games the ball changes hands quite often. If a team loses possession, they will get it back quickly anyway.

At what age do you start to introduce more tactical awareness?
They start really once they are comfortable with the ball. Once they can do what we expect of them technically, we start introducing them to the stage of relating themselves to another player, then relating to three and four other players. Finally, we start to build a clear picture of how to play within a team.

When they get to the U14 – U16 ages, what are they being taught?
By the U14 age they should be getting a good grasp of the tactical considerations and are being taught the different relationships of players and how to react to what other players do around them. By the U16 age they should be at the stage where we want to sign them as full-time youth players. At the U17 – U19 age group, there shouldn't be too many new things for them to learn, it's just that they will be training full-time and training with a little more depth and detail and certainly the training will be a little more demanding. With the full-time youth players (U17 – U19), I also feel it is extremely important to make sure they have good technique and make sure it can stand up under pressure.

What about video analysis?
I would love to have that capability. Unfortunately, we don't have it yet. I have explored it, and when our Academy opens I would like to have a video suite and camera towers over the training fields. Right now, we don't have the facilities available to us. Occasionally, I will show the players video highlights from various games to get certain points across.

How often do you work on finishing and shooting?
We tend to do finishing sessions when the goalkeeper coach is working with the goalkeeper. I don't like the

Interview With Alan Irvine

goalkeeper just being cannon fodder and having shot after shot blasted at him. When we do finishing, I like it to be with movement and not just a pass followed by a shot. I like to have defenders involved to make it more game realistic. Obviously, we do shooting sessions unopposed so the players can concentrate purely on technique, however, I like to move on to more realistic situations with defenders if possible.

How often do you work on set-plays?
We will usually work on set-plays in the morning before a game. We have a number of corner-kicks, free-kicks and throw-ins that we have worked on earlier in the season and the morning before a game we will just brush-up on them.

How does the physical size of a player affect whether a player is selected for one of the younger teams?
At age 15, I was only five foot tall and was turned down by several professional clubs because I was considered undersized. Therefore, I am very sympathetic toward smaller players. A small player may not be that effective right now, but I look to see if he is intelligent, if he has good ability, if he is good technically, if he has got quick feet and does he have good vision? In other words, I try to look at what he will develop into rather than how effective he is

right now. The other thing to realize is that for a smaller player to play with other players who are physically bigger than he is, he is going to need to have a better touch on the ball and his tactical awareness has to be better, just so he can survive.

Also, you have to look at the physically larger player and ask why is he successful. Is he successful because he has a good touch, good skills and is tactically sound? Or is he good because he is bigger and stronger than most other players he plays with and against?

When did you make the transition from playing to coaching?
While I was playing at Blackburn Rovers and started to get involved with the youth players and the Academy. I had already taken coaching licenses in England and Scotland. I then got a long-term injury breaking my collarbone and dislocating my shoulder. Kenny Dalglish, who was the manager at the time, offered me a full-time position working with the youth players. It was a difficult decision to retire from playing, but it was also a great opportunity to step into the coaching ranks.

Alan Irvine - Playing With A 3-5-2

Alan Irvine believes in giving players the responsibility and freedom to be able to make decisions for themselves on the field. We discussed playing with a 3-5-2 formation where most teams play with a holding defensive midfield player to help the three-man defense. Irvine would rather play with what he describes as a more flexible system where the defenders and midfielders have 'partnerships' with each other and react depending on the many various situations that can arise during a game

Partnerships
In diagram 1, the players are organized with three defenders and five midfielders. The main partnerships are:

D1 with M1
D2 with M2
D3 with M3

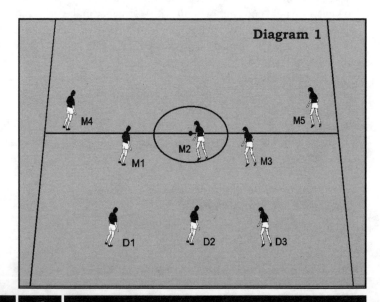

Diagram 1

Alan Irvine - Playing With A 3-5-2

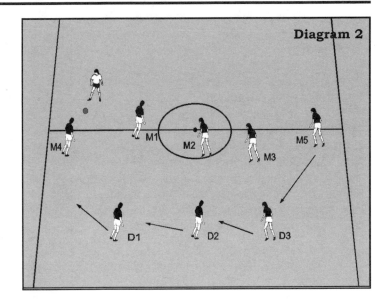

Diagram 2

Partnerships - Defending

If M4 is attacked, then D1 moves over to provide cover. D2 should slide over to take D1's position. D3 should slide over to take D2's position.

M5 drops back to take D3's position.

This makes a four-man defense when the team is not in possession of the ball.

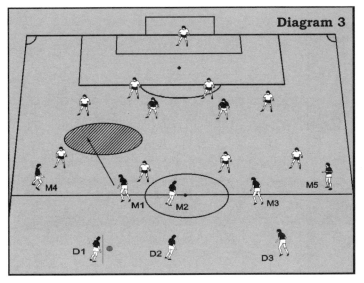

Diagram 3

Partnerships - Attacking

If D1 has the ball, then his partner, M1, should make an angled run into the space between the opposition's midfielders and defenders.

Partnerships - Attacking

If M1 is tracked back by his marker, it allows D1 the space to pass at angles to his teammates.

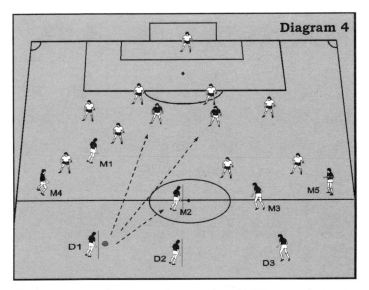

Diagram 4

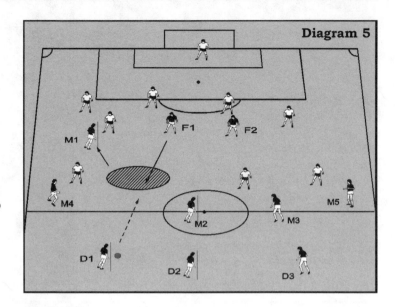

Diagram 5

Partnerships - Attacking

If M1 is tracked back by his marker, he could continue moving forward all the way to the opposition's defending line taking his marker with him. This would leave space for a forward, F1, to check back into, and receive a pass from D1. This can be quite effective because the defender marking F1 would be uncomfortable following F1 that far up field and leaving too much space behind him.

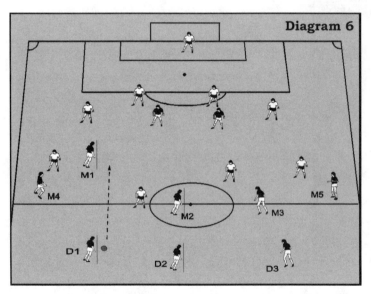

Diagram 6

Partnerships - Attacking

If M1 is not tracked by his marker who instead stays and pressures D1 with the ball, then this allows D1 to pass to M1 who is unmarked and should have plenty of space to receive the ball.

U.S. Women's World Cup Team

Observed October 5 in Kansas City. Following their success in the Women's World Cup and my earlier interview with head coach, Tony DiCicco, I was excited to have the opportunity to watch the U.S. Women's team and its coaches during a practice prior to their upcoming game in Kansas City against Finland.

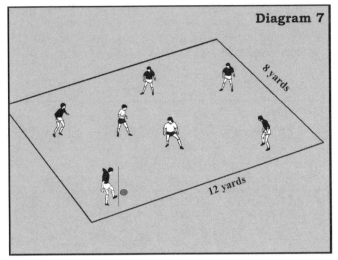

Diagram 7

Warm-Up

Following a 15-minute individual warm-up and stretch, the players did a formal warm-up with the conditioning coach.

5 v 2 Keep-Away

Assistant coach Lauren Gregg then continued the warm-up with two groups of 5 v 2 one-touch keep-away in a 12 x 8-yard area. The player responsible for losing possession alternated with the defender who won possession.

Progression

One touch ariel keep-away with the players juggling the ball in the air.

Heading Game

The players split into groups of four and played 2 v 2 in the same 12 x 8-yard area. The object of the game was for players A and B to head the ball back and forth to each other while advancing to the end-line of players C and D. To score a goal, A or B had to head the ball across C and D's end-line. When not in possession, C and D retreat back to their end-line and one player acts as a goalkeeper and can use their hands. If a team lets the ball hits the ground, then possession goes to the other team.

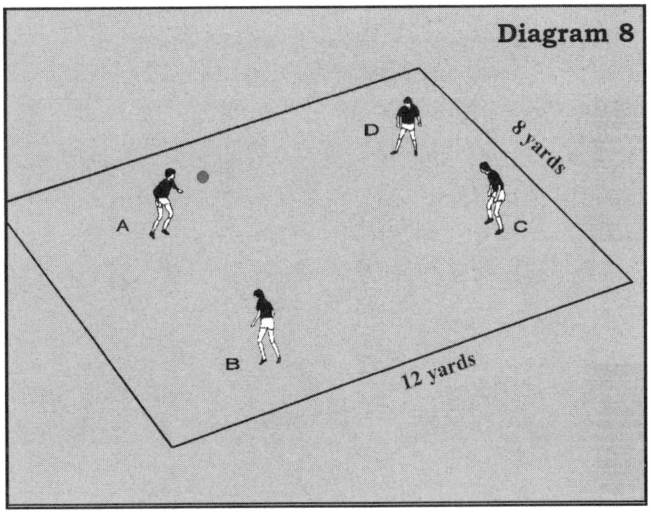

Diagram 8

Soccer Volleyball

Two groups played at the same time. Each group consisted of 4 v 4 plus a goalkeeper in each team. The game is played similar to volleyball. The coach positions himself at the center and serves a ball in the air to one team. That team must then get the ball to the opposite side over an imaginary net using no more than three touches and without letting the ball hit the ground. (The coach is responsible for determining and ruling if the ball went over the imaginary net.) When a team wins a point, the coach moves down field five yards. The objective of the game is to keep moving the net toward your opponent's end-line and win the game.

The goalkeeper has the choice of using her feet or punching the ball.

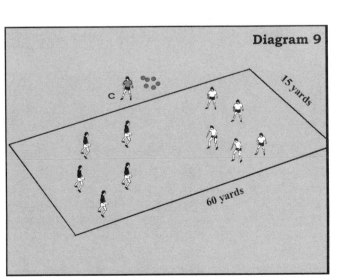

Diagram 9

Full-Field Game

Coach Tony DiCicco then spent 20 minutes working with the team with the following set-up. The field was set up with one goal on the edge of the penalty area as shown in diagram 10. The field was then split into three even sections. In one end, the three starting defenders played against the three starting forwards. In the middle third, the midfielders played 2 v 2 plus a neutral player that played for the team in possession. The other end had two defenders against two forwards. The players had to stay in their own third of the field except for a midfielder who could join the attacking third once the ball was passed in. The forwards could pass the ball back to a teammate into the middle third if they had no other options on offense.

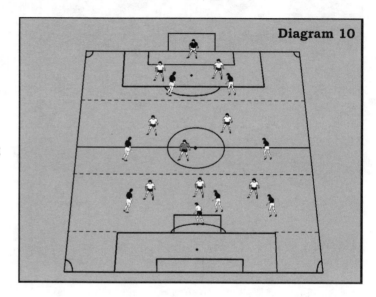

Diagram 10

Coach DiCicco would stop the game occasionally to get a point across, otherwise the players were allowed to play without restrictions.

The game progressed to a 7 v 7 + 1 game on the same field, except the field was narrowed both sides by five yards. Again, the starting forwards and starting defenders were on opposite teams.

Practice ended with the players having 15 minutes of free time to work on shooting, restarts, etc. Some players did sit-ups or spent their time stretching.

D.C. United - Conditioning

A pre-season conditioning practice observed at Myrtle Beach, February 1999.

Conditioning Runs

The field is marked with three separate tracks of cones marked from one end of the field to the other and back again. Each set of cones requires the players to run at varying speeds up to a maximum of 75%. To make them easier to read they are shown here in separate diagrams (11,1 2 and 13). Eight players line up in pairs at each station and perform three complete runs (there and back). After completing three runs, followed by two minutes rest, each group of players rotate so they complete each set of cones.

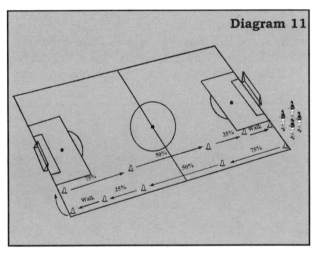

Station One

Sprint at 75% pace for 35 yards.
Run at 50% pace for 35 yards.
Jog at 25% pace for 20 yards.
Walk for 18 yards.
Repeat going back to starting line.
Complete three cycles.

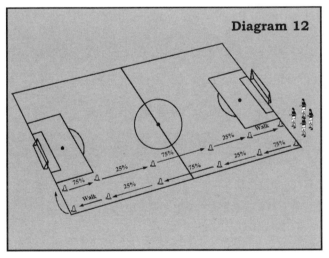

Station Two

Sprint at 75% pace for 20 yards.
Jog at 25% pace for 20 yards.
Sprint at 75% pace for 25 yards.
Jog at 25% pace for 20 yards.
Walk for 20 yards.
Repeat going back to the starting line.
Complete three cycles.

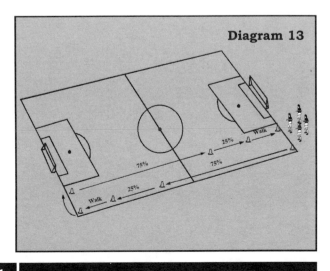

Station Three

Sprint at 75% pace for 70 yards.
Jog at 25% pace for 20 yards.
Walk for 18 yards.
Repeat going back to the starting line.
Complete three cycles.

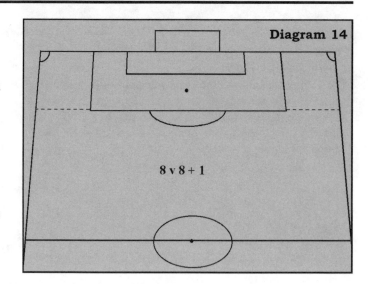

Diagram 14

8 v 8 + 1

Possession

Play 8 v 8 plus one neutral player who plays for the team in possession.

- Play two touch keep-away for three minutes then rest for two minutes
- Play one touch keep-away for three minutes then rest for two minutes
- Then have each player pair up with someone from the opposite team. Play four minutes of unlimited touches keep-away. Each player can only tackle his partner.

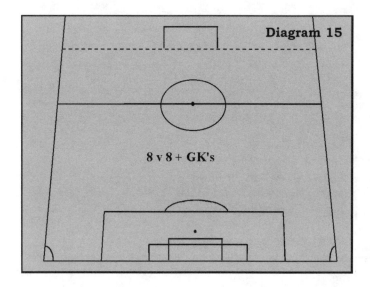

Diagram 15

8 v 8 + GK's

3/4 Field Game

Place a goal 35 yards from one goal-line to make a 3/4 size field. Play 8 v 8 plus goalkeepers.

- Play unlimited touches for five minutes followed by one minute rest
- Play two touch for five minutes followed by one minute rest
- Play unlimited touches for five minutes

End practice with 10 minutes of light jogging and stretching

Contributed by coach Nicu Lazar of F.C. Petrolul Ploiesti of the Romanian First Division.

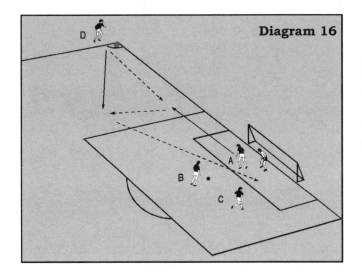

Diagram 16

Corner Kick One

Player A sprints toward the corner.
Player D passes him the ball and makes an angled run toward the corner of the penalty area.
Player A passes one touch to player D.
Player D has two options; shooting high toward the far post or crossing to the far post for players B and C.

Coaching Points

- One touch passes due to the lack of time and space
- If shooting, hit with the inside of the foot to bend the ball into the far post
- Precise accurate passes

Corner Kick Two

The same set up as in Corner Kick One. This time, when player A receives the ball, he turns with the outside of his foot and has two options:
A. Dribble into the six-yard box to shoot or pass
B. Cross after turning

Coaching Points

- Quick one touch turn
- If player A decides to pass, he must attempt to draw one or more defenders to him before he passes
- The pass must be at an angle away from the goalkeeper

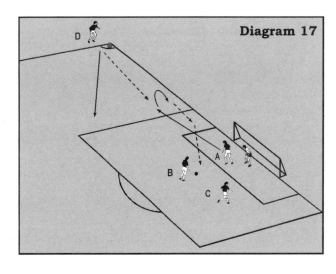

Diagram 17

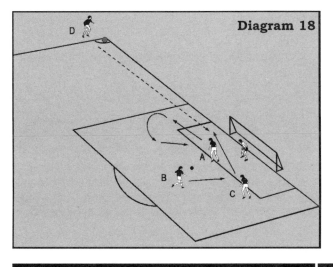

Diagram 18

Corner Kick Three

This time player A sprints toward the corner then checks away and continues his run back toward the goal.
Player C moves quickly into player A's starting position.
Player D delivers the corner kick to the near post for player C to flick on to incoming players A and B.

Coaching Points

- The timing of the runs is critical
- The corner kick must be a firm driven cross

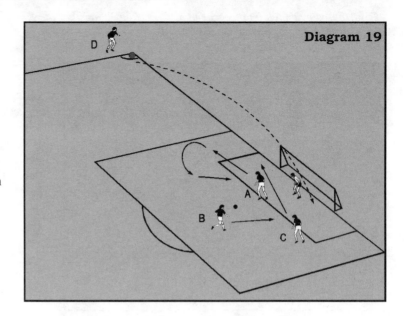

Diagram 19

Corner Kick Four

The same set up and player movement as in Corner Kick Three. This time the corner kick is delivered to the far post for a direct header/shot on goal or the ball can be redirected across the goal.

Coaching Points for all Corner Kicks

- Start with unopposed practice then add defenders to make it more game realistic
- All the corner kicks start with the same player positioning. This makes it extremely difficult for the defending team to guess what kind of corner kick you are doing
- Drill them regularly until the players understand the positioning and how they are executed, then practice them in a friendly game or against defenders that haven't seen the corner kicks in practice
- Include signals so your players know which corner kick you are doing

Mike Smith

Mike Smith is one of the world's most experienced international coaches. To date he has coached teams in 212 international games. From 1974 to 1980 he was the manager of the Welsh National Team. From 1985 to 1988 he was manager of the Egypt National team where he won the African Nations Cup and the African Olympics. Currently, Mike is at Wolverhampton Wanderers of the English First Division where he works with the youth team players.

Change of Possession - Time to Counter Attack

Of the three main aspects of soccer, dealing with 'change of possession' is the most difficult. If we only use attack versus defense practices, play can become predictable. Defense versus attack sessions usually result in the defenders dominating and everything becomes repetitive. Even if we overload the attackers in the sessions, it becomes difficult to recreate game conditions due to the pace and starting position of the defenders. Therefore, when players have the space, they should be encouraged to run with the ball. Then a decision needs to made at the end of the run:

Can you score?
Do you cross the ball?
Do you pass the ball?
Does the run change into a dribble?

But some players, however fast they are, don't have the fakes and moves to beat a defender consistently. These players need to create a 2 v 1 situation with a teammate to beat an opponent. The extra player offers several alternatives in beating a defender. These players need to see opportunities and the extra players need to make the correct supporting runs.

If we keep these conditions to run at opponents, we are expecting the players to have knowledge of other positions/ roles. For instance, a center midfielder swaps passes with a forward but is forced wide. He then has to assume the responsibilities of the wide player. Good players can cope with rotation of positions but decisions can be very difficult.

To re-emphasize; the three main aspects of soccer are:

When a team is possession
When a team is not in possession
When possession changes

Change of possession can happen at any time, on any part of the field. (Over 300 times during a professional game.)

A change of possession is a great time to run at opponents because the other team will probably have pushed up to support their attack. Once you have won possession and started running at your opponents, it is essential that teammates break out fast either into position to receive a pass or close up to support the player on the ball.

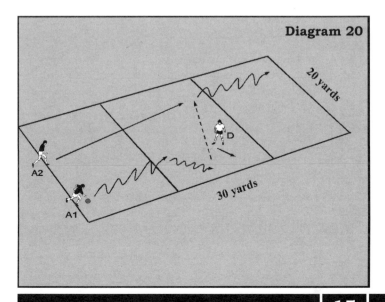

Diagram 20

20 yards

30 yards

A2

A1

D

Developing in Grids
Player A1 runs with the ball at pace through the first grid and moves to his right as he approaches the defender, D.
Player A2 runs at speed to support player A1.
Player A1 can pass to player A2 to beat the defender.

Coaching Points
- This exercise is very basic, but the angle of support offered to player A1 is very important
- The further player A1 drags the defender to the right, (away from his supporting run) the easier it will be to connect with the pass

Mike Smith

Coaching Points

As a coach, it is important to pay attention to detail and refer back to the grid and examine all the essential factors. For instance, it is important that player A2 lets player A1 know he is running in support. In the middle third of the grid, decisions need to be made at pace so player A1 needs to slow slightly to ensure he has full control of the ball and he is able to fully engage the defender. At that point, he must decide on his best option. The objective is for players A1 and A2 to get past the defender. This offers the coach the opportunity to challenge players A1 and A2 using the 'Show Me' guided discovery method.

Coaching Observations

- Does player A1 have a fake or move to beat the defender?
- Does player A1 have a change of pace to run past the defender?
- Does player A1 play the pass flat and allow player A2 to run past the defender or does he play the ball behind the defender for player A1 to run on to?

Progression

Using the same field, progress the exercise by playing 3 v 1 in one end third of the field and 2 v 1 in the other end third of the field. The middle third of the field is empty. The ball starts in the end third with the 3 v 1. The three attackers pass the ball until one of them has an opportunity and space to run with the ball. The objective is to run to the opposite end third of the field and keep possession once in that third to continue the exercise.

Progression

Play 3 v 2 in each end third with a passive defender in the middle third.

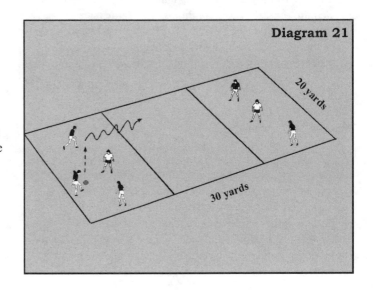

Diagram 21

Three v Three

To develop the practice, play 3 v 3, the smallest numbered game to produce and reproduce triangles. It also puts into practice the various decisions the player in possession needs to make.

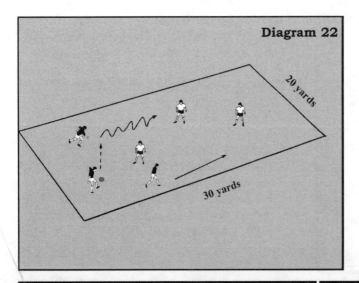

Diagram 22

In this game, the third player is significant because his runs, either near, wide or long, would give the passing option needed by the player in possession to get past the three defenders.

Because the game is continuous, any interception changes the game. So the team not in possession has to work hard not only defending but in trying to win tackles or intercept a pass.

Coaching Point

As possession is lost, all decisions change - good players will show that they can solve the situations they face.

Mike Smith

Half-Field Game

Coaches should develop all the previous situations in a variety of games. Playing 6 v 6 or 7 v 7 across half a field will produce many situations for the coach to observe and develop. Don't have offside in effect but protect the goalkeepers by insisting on one touch finishing only. The players are encouraged to run with the ball when they get the opportunity.

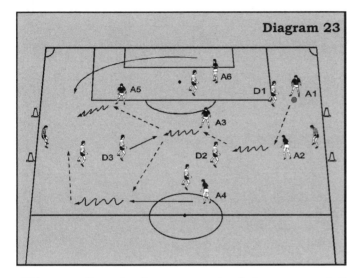

Diagram 23

In the example in diagram 23, A1 passes to A2.
A2 has space so he runs with the ball at D2 and makes a decision to pass to A3, A4 or continue his dribble. In this example he passes to A3.
A3 has space, so he runs forward and is defended by D3. Again, a decision has to be made. A3 can continue to dribble or pass wide to A4 or A5.
If A5 receives the ball, he can attack the goal and shoot.
If A4 receives the ball he can attack the end-line and deliver a low hard cross.

This game allows the players to examine their route to goal. However, if the A players lose possession, the B players must now attack by running the ball out of defense at opposing players. Then the question is, how do the A players respond? Do they run back? Where do they run to?

Coaching Point

The speed of movement of the counter-attack is critical in giving the attack by the B players superior numbers and exposing the A players.

Conclusion

- Many small-sided games are used to improve the technical qualities of the first touch, passing, support, movement, etc. But not many games are focused on running with the ball and attacking your opponents quickly.
- Most small-sided games are neat and tidy, mistakes are rare and usually involve play around the 'final pass'.
- Change the focus for the players so that not only do they have to win or intercept the ball, they then have to travel with it as fast as possible into the spaces that are available.
- Communication is vital because every player on each team must recognize their role at any moment of the game.
- I work with 15-16 year old players who really get up a 'head of steam' during these sessions.
- This session has all the decisions you will find in a game and they are recreated in a controlled way.

Dallas Burn

Observed in Florida, February 2000 during pre-season training. The main part of the session was focused on restarts. It was a little windy with the temperature in the mid 70's.

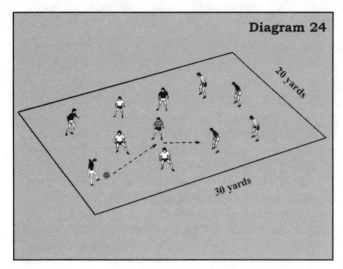

Diagram 24

Warm-up
After 20 minutes of jogging and stretching, the players split into two groups, each in a 20 x 30-yard area and played 5 v 5 + 1 keep-away.

Play three 2-minute games and stretch for two minutes in between.

Offensive Corner Kicks
The players stayed in the same two groups and practiced various unopposed corner kicks. All variations were practiced from both flanks for a total of 20 minutes.

The set up in diagram 25 is used for practicing near post corner kicks with player G attempting to flick the ball on for players A, B and C to run on to.

Coaching Point
If players A, B and C didn't have a clear shooting chance, the ball was laid back to players D and E who shot on goal with one touch.

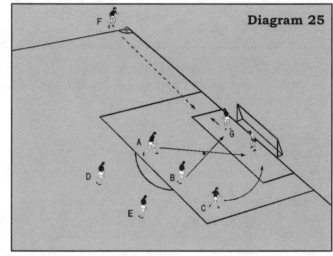

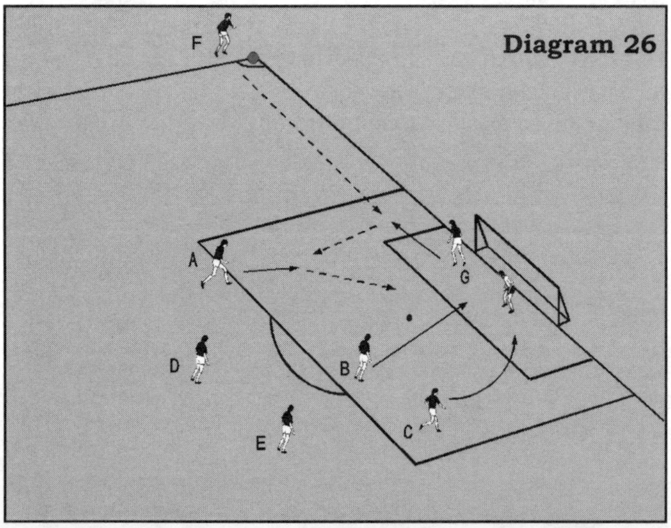

Diagram 25

Offensive Corner Kicks
The set up was the same as in diagram 25 with the exception of player A, who's starting position was more toward the corner of the penalty area. Instead of driving the ball for player G to flick with his head, it was played to his feet. Player G then laid the ball back with one touch for player A to shoot or cross.

Diagram 26

Dallas Burn

Diagram 27

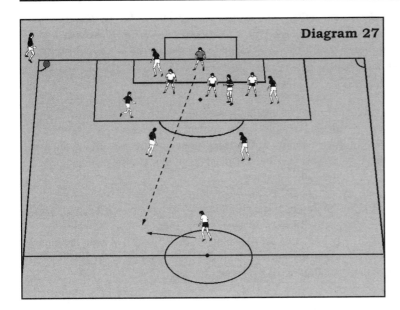

Offensive and Defensive Corner Kicks

Three defenders are introduced to make the exercise more game-realistic. Also, a forward for the defending team is positioned near the half-line. The objective for the defenders is to clear the ball as far as possible for the forward to try and get on the end of the clearance. If the goalkeeper got the ball, he made a quick throw to the forward (as in diagram 25).

Coaching Point

Each time the ball was cleared or thrown by the goalkeeper, the three defenders pushed upfield forcing the forwards to follow or remain in an offside position.

Following the corner kicks, the players practiced crossing the ball 10 yards from the end-line using the same set up and number of players. This was followed by 15 minutes practicing various restarts from about 20-30 yards from goal.

Practice ended with the players stretching individually for 5-10 minutes. Some players continued to work on shooting situations from around the box trying to bend the ball round a wall.

PSV Eindhoven

Contributed by subscriber, Alan Maher. Alan has coached at the college and high school level. He has written articles for the NSCAA Soccer Journal, Southern Soccer Scene and the New York Times. Alan has been visiting Holland for over 20 years and has observed the training sessions of many Dutch teams. This article is taken from a conversation with Tony Bruin Slot, head of youth training for PSV Eindhoven.

I have travelled to Holland for more than twenty years. Normally I watch the training and games of the first team of a professional club. For a change of pace I visited PSV Eindhoven one recent September and watched the youth teams train and play games. I was lucky enough to be introduced to Tony Bruin Slot who was the head of the youth program and world wide scouting. A busy man.

Tony gave us more than two hours of his time on this day. I asked him two questions and his response took up the two hours. He used a chalk board to illustrate his program. The phone rang the whole time that we were there. He ignored the phone and lectured on a subject that we knew was dear to his heart. He had spent a little over eleven years working with Johan Cruyff and he wanted to deliver the message to us. It was a complete system, as we soon learned, and one that he wanted to share with us. We took no notes, so we relied on memory. His message:

Team formation: PSV likes the youth teams to play a 3-4-3 formation. And the team should be compact enough to allow the back line player to make a direct pass to the front line player. As the front line runs up the field, the back line must advance at the same rate so the two lines are connected. This formation creates many triangles and the connected triangles create diamonds all over the field. As a result, the youth players are taught to visualize triangles.

This means that upon receiving a pass, the player with the ball should see two potential receivers of a pass. The visualization of the triangle needs to be done before the ball is received. Players must be prepared to receive and pass the ball.

Passing patterns: The players were not encouraged to cross the ball from one flank to the other. Rather, the ball was passed up a central spine or up the flanks. Again, the back and front lines were always close enough to provide one touch passing from one line to the other.

Recruiting: PSV is in an ideal location in Holland. As a result, players from both Germany and Belgium cross the border to play with the club. Also, the high organization of the program is attractive and draws players from all over the area. On a day of training, the players train for an hour and rest for an hour followed by another hour of training. During the resting time, the players can attend to homework for school or just rest.

Style of play: The program has developed a distinct style of play. We will try to cover some of the various aspects:

• Stagger the central spine. This is done to encourage passes that skip the middle line.

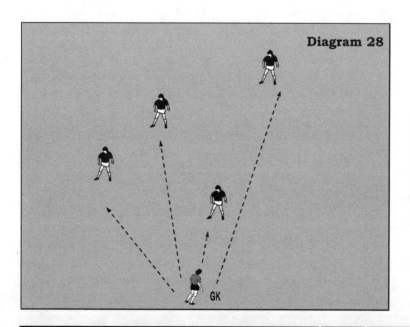

Diagram 28

Staggered Spine
Looking from the goalkeeper, he should be able to see all the players. The result is that three players never stand in a straight line in any direction on any part of the field. This encourages the passes to skip a line of players and advance the ball as quickly as possible.

PSV Eindhoven

• Pass the ball and follow the pass. PSV does not want players to pass and stand. Go to the ball. Give support to the player receiving the ball. Move up. Everybody move up. Rinus Michels used to say, "Go to the ball!"

• Get behind your opponent's rear end. But do not run into an offside position!

• Prepare to receive the ball. This is done by turning the body to face the direction in which the ball will be played. As the old saying goes, "Pass the way that you are facing." Face that way in advance. Do not wait to receive the ball and then turn.

• Always see the third player. This means that the player receiving the ball should avoid passing the ball back to the player who delivered the pass. Pass the ball on to a new player - the third player. Avoid back passing to the first player.

• Compact the team on half the field. This is essential on the defense. The team needs to shut down passing channels and deny space to the opponents. When the ball is on the flank, the team should also compact to the ball side of the field. This is risky, but the Dutch like to take risks.

• Discourage dribbling except in the final third of the field. And passes should be to feet, not space.

• The principles of play can be learned by playing 7 v 7 or 8 v 8.

• Stress depth before width. See comments above about compacting.

• Do everything with the ball.

• Stop play and ask why passes were made. Players need to be held responsible for what they do on the field of play.

• Remember that technique comes before tactics. Do not try to conceal poor technique by players with an elaborate system of play.

• Movement off the ball is critical. Only one player has the ball; the rest cannot stand around and watch the one player. This also means frequent movement of the ball to force movement off the ball. The two go together.

Players are selected according to:

Technical ability
Speed of the player
Tactical ability
Personality/mental ability

Winning is less important than developing the team as a single unit.

Half of each team was composed of players at the proper age. The other half were one year below that age. Year by year this changed of course.

Some final notes:
The youth program is one that is filled with patience. The prime emphasis is on the team organization with rapid movement of the ball and proper movement off the ball. Winning is less important than developing the team as a single unit. The team must learn to play together before it can be expected to win. During the game, the coaches make few comments. Technique is ignored; only tactics are addressed, and only for the first few minutes of the game.

Parents are given lessons about how to behave during a game. They are rather quiet and cheer good play, not the work done by their own child. They make no comments about technique. They learn how to really watch a game of soccer.

We watched many youth games. They were all well played in a rather quiet atmosphere. We were able to concentrate on the game. There were no distracting noises. Soccer is taken seriously in Holland. PSV is very serious about the youth program. As I write this, PSV has again won the championship. It was expected.

FK Teplice - Youth Team

Contributed by Scott Placek, Director of Senior Programs, Longhorns Soccer Club, Austin, TX.

This training session is from the journal I compiled during my trip to Teplice, Czech Republic. From March 14 - 22, 2000, I visited FK Teplice, a professional club in the Czech Gambrinus Liga (1st Division). The purpose of my visit was to observe the training methods and philosophies that form the basis for youth soccer development in the Czech Republic. During my visit, I was hosted by Mr.. Roman Vlk, the director of the FK Teplice youth teams, and a fully qualified coach with the Czech F.A.

Mr.. Vlk and FK Teplice were most helpful during my visit.

I was able to attend training sessions for many of the youth teams and spent time individually with Mr.. Vlk to discuss training philosophy and structures for youth teams in the Czech Republic. The observations in this journal are my interpretations of the things I saw. I have tried to record the training sessions precisely as they occurred.

I wish to thank Roman Vlk and the staff of FK Teplice for hosting me and providing me unfettered access to the teams and training sessions. I could not have wished for a better experience, or nicer people to meet.

A Zaci (1985) Training Session

The A Záci squad is trained by a young former player whose career was ended by injury. He was assisted by Roman Vlk and the assistant trainer. The session lasted 80 minutes. Seventeen players were present including two goalkeepers. For the first five minutes, the players warmed up on their own, primarily with juggling and dribbling. There was very little stoppage or talking going on. If a ball got away, the player hurried to get it back and start warming up again.

Warm-up
For the next 10 minutes the trainer put the team through a directed warm-up with the team moving across the width of the field in a line. Each player had a ball which was incorporated into the warm-up, including some exercises where the ball was handled for variety. Between exercises, dynamic stretching was used.

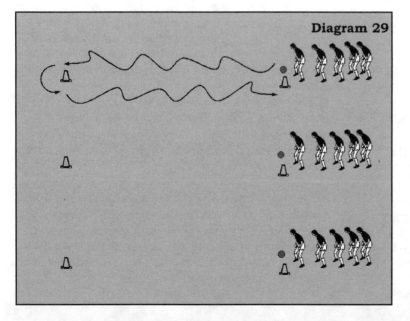

Diagram 29

Technical Work - Speed & Accuracy
The next segment of the training involved relay races for three teams of five. (The goalkeepers were working with the club trainer at this time.)

Each team of five players lined up behind a cone, with another cone placed 15 - 20 yards away.

Speed dribble around the far cone and speed dribble back to the next player in line. One time through line. This race was run three times.

NOTE: In each of the following races, the last placed team was "punished" with some sort of jumping exercises – five jumps for each player then the next race was started. This gave the exercises an edge of friendly competition, as the teams urged their members on and gave some good-natured joking to the losing team.

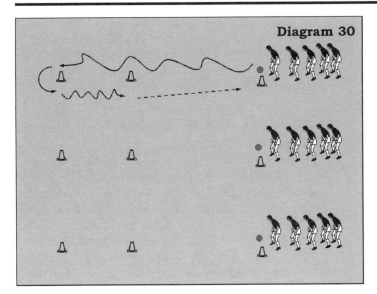

Diagram 30

Progression

Now a third cone was placed between the two existing cones, slightly closer to the far end, but nearer the middle. Now the relay was run by speed dribble around the far cone and a return pass at the middle cone. This race was run three times. I noticed that the passes were unusually crisp. There is a great confidence in the ability of their teammates to control the ball. Still, the first touch was lacking a little and some balls got away.

Progression

The next race was to dribble a circle around the middle cone then continue to and around the far cone and speed dribble back to the line. Again this race was done three times.

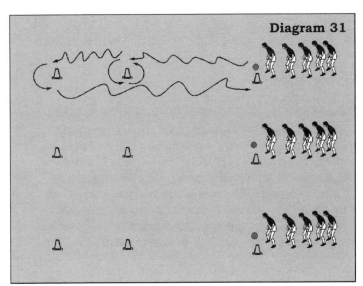

Diagram 31

Diagram 32

Progression

The next race was speed dribble to the middle cone, turning back, (not rounding the cone) and speed dribble to the starting cone, turning again to speed dribble around the far cone with the ball and pass back to the next player in line after rounding the far cone. Again this race was done three times.

Circuit Training

Next the three teams were put into three stations for circuit training that lasted about 10 minutes at each station before the groups rotated. One trainer worked each station.

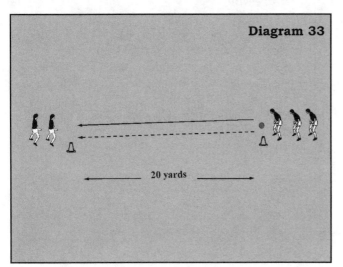

Diagram 33

20 yards

Station One - Passing

This station, for the first five minutes, featured the players facing each other in single file lines at cones 20 yards apart. The starting player passed the ball down to the other player and SPRINTED to the other line. Players had one touch to receive and were expected to play the pass on the next touch. The passes were solid and accurate for the most part. The players worked very hard, taking the admonition to sprint to the other line very seriously.

Progression

After five minutes the trainer added two cones in front of each of the end cones. The end cone became the point of a triangle. The base of the triangle was about 4 yards wide, and the end cones about 3 yards at an angle from the point. The starting player was expected to pass the ball between the base cones to a player stepping inside the triangle to receive. The receiving player was then to take a first touch that put the ball outside the base cones and play the pass into the base on the opposite side. Again, players sprinted to the other side after passing. Technique and accuracy broke down a little over this demand.

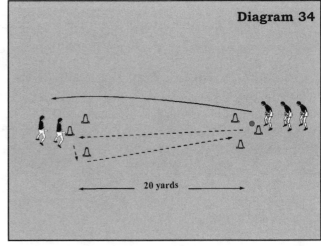

Diagram 34

20 yards

Diagram 35

30 yards

Station Two - Shooting

The goalkeepers rotated in this station. The trainer set up three flags in a single file line starting about 20 yards from goal and spaced about two yards apart. The players started about 10 yards from the flag, dribbled in a weave through the flags and took their shots immediately on clearing the flag with whichever foot the ball was on.

Diagram 36

Station Three - Small sided game

The teams played a 3 v 2 keepaway game without touch limitations. When the defenders were pressing, most of the game was one and two touch. If the defenders tired or eased off on the pressure, the attacking group would slow the play down and hold the ball, forcing the defenders to come to them.

Scrimmage

The session ended with an unrestricted scrimmage game. The total session lasted 80 minutes.

FK Teplice

Contributed by Scott Placek, Director of Senior Programs, Longhorns Soccer Club, Austin, TX. In the September/ October issue we looked at the training session of the FK Teplice U15 Youth Team. This article is from a training session of the U18 Youth Team. You can find more about Scott's visit to the Czech Republic on his web site http: //soccer.placek.com

This training session is from the journal I compiled during my trip to Teplice, Czech Republic. From March 14 - 22, 2000, I visited FK Teplice, a professional club in the Czech Gambrinus Liga (1st Division). The purpose of my visit was to observe the training methods and philosophies that form the basis for youth soccer development in the Czech Republic. During my visit, I was hosted by Mr.. Roman Vlk, the director of the FK Teplice youth teams, and a fully qualified coach with the Czech F.A.

Mr.. Vlk and FK Teplice were most helpful during my visit.

I was able to attend training sessions for many of the youth teams and spent time individually with Mr.. Vlk to discuss training philosophy and structures for youth teams in the Czech Republic. The observations in this journal are my interpretations of the things I saw. I have tried to record the training sessions precisely as they occurred.

I wish to thank Roman Vlk and the staff of FK Teplice for hosting me and providing me unfettered access to the teams and training sessions. I could not have wished for a better experience, or nicer people to meet.

A Dorost (1981/82) Training Session

This session was conducted by the trainer for the "A Dorost team". There were 17 players, including two goalkeepers. The players took the field before the coach, carried the equipment to the pitch and immediately started to warm themselves up with passing and moving with 6 or 7 balls across half the field. The warm up was serious with very little stoppage or talking, except to ask for a ball. When the coaches arrived, the assistant trainer took the goalkeepers to work with them and the coach divided the remaining 15 players into groups of three.

Warm-Up - Groups of Three

A. The players performed a three man weave across half the field. The formation of the players was tight and passes were played with one touch.

B. Juggling - Each group was asked to keep the ball in the air, working with their feet first and then just their heads.

C. Passing - Each group of players was organized in a line spaced about 12 yards apart, with the players on the end facing each other as shown in diagram 1. There was one ball per group. The player in the middle faced the player with the ball. The ball was played into him. He turned with one touch and then passed the ball to the opposite player on his next touch. Players performed for 30 seconds and then switched. This rotation was repeated several times through.

Coaching Points
- The player in the middle was always moving toward the ball to receive
- The coach had to challenge the players to work quickly to receive and quickly to turn - He jumped into one group and demonstrated what he wanted, the players picked up their pace after that
- Every pass was hit with good pace and received comfortably

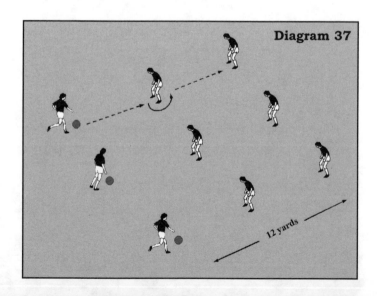

Diagram 37

12 yards

Progressions

- Inside of Foot Volleys - Using the same set up as in diagram 1, but with a ball at each end player, the player in the middle received a thrown ball and volleyed it back with the inside of the foot, turned and received from the next player and repeated for a 30 second rotation. In this exercise, the emphasis of the coach was again on speed of play, and accuracy wasn't as good, with many players having to chase down miss-hit balls.
- Heading - Using the same set up, the ball was served in to be returned with the head. The serves were designed to make the player jump into the air to head the ball. Problems with accuracy continued, though the coach was satisfied with the pace.

Circuit Training

Seven stations were set up for the players to work at. The players paired up and worked each station for 20 seconds, then rested as their partner worked. After two work sessions per player, the groups rotated stations.

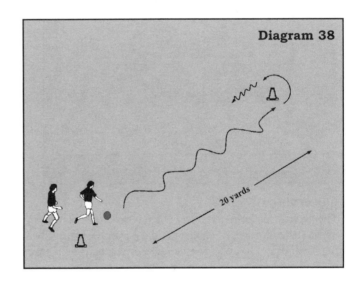

Diagram 38

Station One

Five gates ranging in height from 18 to 24 inches are lined up in a row with no more than a yard between each. The players do high knee jumps straight over the gates and back, bringing their knees up toward their chest.

Station Two

Two cones are placed 20 yards apart as shown in diagram 38. The players do speed dribbling from one cone to the other and back for duration of work period.

Station Three

The players do abdominal crunches with feet held up off the ground.

Station Four

Using a single gate about 24 inches high, the players do high knee jumps side to side over the gate.

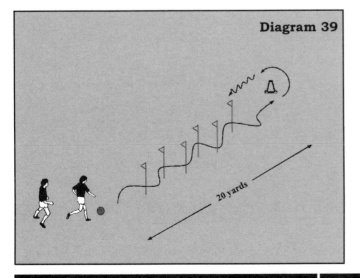

Diagram 39

Station Five

Six flag poles are placed two yards apart as shown in diagram 39. The players run a dribble weave through cones and back.

FK Teplice

Station Six

Fourteen hurdles about 9 - 12 inches off the ground are placed close together. The players run over and back lifting their feet high to clear the hurdles.

Station Seven

Two cones are placed 15 yards apart. The players do shuttle runs from cone to cone for duration of work period.

The team made three rounds through the circuits. Between each round the team did light jogging and static stretching and took good rest periods.

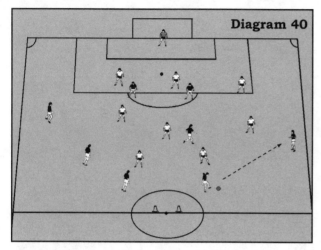

Diagram 40

Field Training

Play 8 v 8 + GK on a half field. The dark team of eight attack the goal with the goalkeeper and the white team of eight attack a small three yard goal made of cones, which does not have a keeper. This was played for about 15 minutes and then was changed to 8 v 6 + GK.

Observations

The players were not given any touch restrictions, but played rather quickly. The players worked very quickly to free a teammate into space. Once free, the player quickly pushed the ball forward. The teams seemed to be looking for opportunities to score from either low driven balls which were played backwards or were sent in diagonally to players making hard diagonal runs toward the center of the goal. The players often demonstrated good use of one-touch passing in tight areas to unbalance the defense and free a teammate to play forward.

Sammy Lee

Assistant Manager and First Team Coach at Liverpool F.C., Lee had a stellar playing career winning four League Championships and two European Cups while playing for Liverpool during the years they dominated English and European soccer. During this time Sammy also played many times for the England National Team. Lee's coaching career started with the reserve team at Liverpool F.C. This was followed by a move to coach the First Team squad as an assistant to the manager, Gerard Houllier. His ability to coach and motivate players didn't go unnoticed when Lee was chosen by head coach, Howard Wilkinson to help coach the England U21 National Team for the Euro-2000 U21 Championships.

This session was conducted at the WORLD CLASS COACHING International Coaching Seminar at Connecticut College in June 2000.

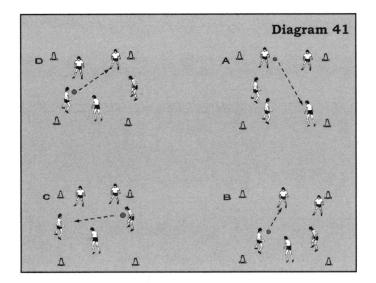

Warm-Up

In an area 30 x 30 yards, work in four 10 x 10-yard areas in the corners as shown in diagram 30 with five players in each area. The players move around their square passing the ball by hand 'basketball' style.

Coaching Point

Encourage good communication.

Warm-Up

On the coach's whistle, the ball is passed clockwise to the next group. For example, group A passes to group B, group B passes to group C, etc.

Coaching Point

Watch for the next ball coming in from the other group and be available to receive it.

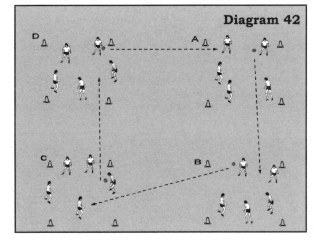

Progressions

Do the same exercise but pass with feet instead of hands. Then progress as before by passing in a clockwise direction from one group to the other. A further progression was added when players followed their pass into the next group.

Every few minutes play was stopped to allow the players to stretch.

Coaching Point

Create angles for the pass out of the box into next one, avoid straight lines.

Sammy Lee

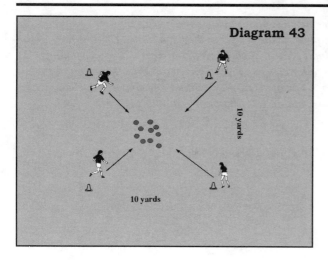

Diagram 43

10 yards

10 yards

Fun Practice Related Game
Organize one player on each cone of a 10 x 10-yard square with 10 balls in the center. The objective is for the players to retrieve the balls from the center of the square with their feet and bring them back to their cone, one ball at a time. The first player to get three balls is the winner. The players may also steal balls from the cones of other players.

Coaching Point
Awareness of where the other balls are in the square.

5 v 3
Mark out two 25 x 25-yard areas side by side as shown in diagram 33. Organize two teams of five. The exercise starts with five dark players playing keep-away from three white players in one of the 25 x 25-yard areas. The other two white players wait in the other 25 x 25-yard area. If the three white players win possession of the ball they move into the other area and join their two teammates. Three players from the dark team follow which creates another 5 v 3 situation this time in the white teams favor.

Coaching Points
- Using a small area ensures the players must make decisions early and be aware of where their next pass is going
- Communication is vital so that the same players are not doing all the work

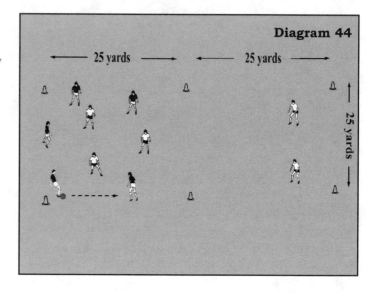

Diagram 44

25 yards

25 yards

25 yards

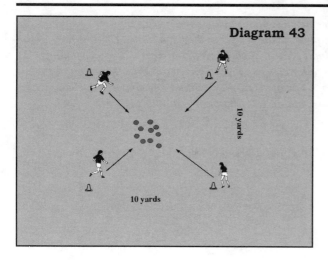

Diagram 45

5 v 3 Breakaway
Using a half field, mark a 15 x 15-yard area on the half-line as shown in diagram 45. Organize two forwards and two defenders on the edge of the penalty area and play 5 v 3 keep-away in the 15 x 15-yard area. When the group of three win possession they quickly collect another ball from outside the area and attack the goal creating a 5 v 2 situation.

Coaching Points
- A quick attack doesn't allow the defenders time to get organized
- Allow only 10 seconds for the attackers to score ensuring quick play

Sammy Lee

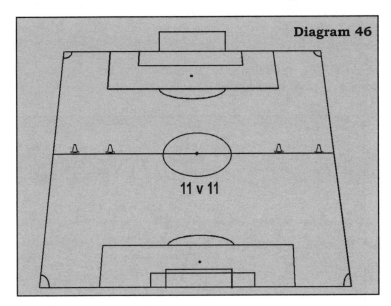

Diagram 46

11 v 11

Full Field Game

Mark two goals with cones or flags on the half-line as shown in diagram 46. Play 11 v 11 using a full field. One team attacks both regular goals and the other team attacks both of the marked goals on the half-line. The team attacking the marked goals score by passing through the goal to a teammate on the other side.

Coaching Points

- Create passing angles
- Look for a forward pass whenever possible
- Quick counter attacking is done over 30-40 yards

Chicago Fire

Observed during pre-season training in Florida, February 2000. This was a morning training session conducted at the time they were practicing twice a day.

Warm-Up/Conditioning

The warm-up consisted of 15 minutes of jogging and stretching. This was followed by 25 minutes of conditioning that included a circuit of sprints weaving in and out of flag poles, over ladders and 40-yard sprints.

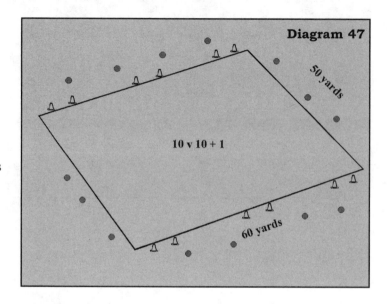

Six Goal Game

Play 10 v 10 on a 50 x 60-yard field with one neutral player that plays for the team in possession. Each team defends three small goals. Have spare balls around the field to keep play moving. If the ball goes out-of-bounds it is put back in play with a kick-in. Play for 20 minutes.

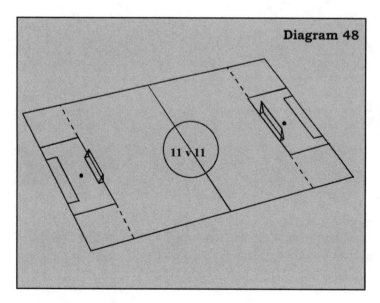

Full-Field Game

Practice ended with an 11 v 11 game on a full field. The goals were set on the 18-yard line. As always with Bob Bradley's practices, the game was very competitive and ended tied at 1-1. This was followed by a 15 minute cool down.

D.C. United

Observed during pre-season training in Florida, February 2000. This session was what coach Thomas Rongen called a "Regeneration Practice". It followed a five-day spell in which the players had played three games. It was a light session with elements of fun, agility and conditioning.

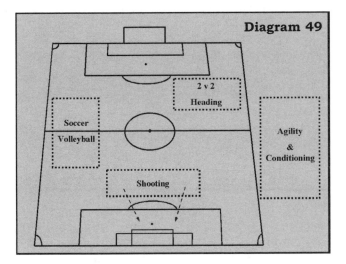

Diagram 49

Warm-Up

The conditioning coach conducted a 20-minute warm-up of jogging and stretching. The players then had five minutes individually to do any further stretches they felt were necessary.

Session Organization

Four stations were set up on a full field as shown in diagram 38. The players were split into four groups of four players. Each station was done for 8 minutes followed by four minutes rest before rotating stations.

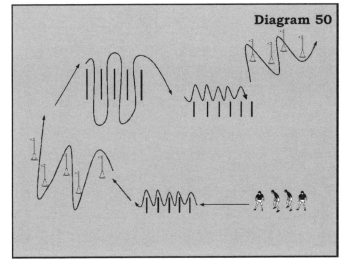

Diagram 50

Agility/Conditioning

The players took turns running over a series of poles, hurdles and around flagpoles. Each player did three circuits with 45 seconds rest between each circuit.

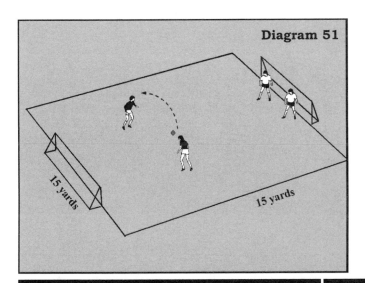

Diagram 51

Heading Game

Play 2 v 2 in a 15 x 15-yard area. The objective of the game is for one pair to keep the ball in the air using only their heads, juggling back and forth while advancing toward their opponent's goal. The two players that are defending must retreat to their goal line. The defending players can use their hands to make a save. If the attacking pair let the ball hit the ground, they lose possession and the other team now attacks.

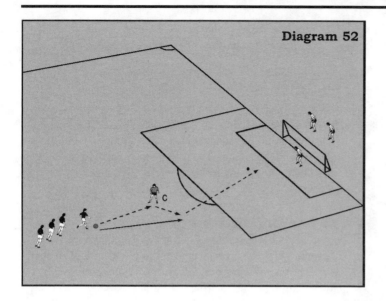

Diagram 52

Finishing

In diagram 34, the players are positioned about 35 yards from goal and a coach is positioned about 25 yards from goal. The first player in line passes to the coach who lays the ball off for the player to shoot. This was done for two minutes and then the coach moved to a position at the corner of the penalty area so the shots were taken from an angle.

The finishing drills also gave the three goalkeepers a workout. The goalkeepers rotated every few shots.

Crossing And Finishing

The last few minutes of the finishing station was a crossing and finishing exercise with a player on each flank receiving balls from the coach and crossing in for the other two players in the penalty area. The coach was also focusing on the goalkeepers who were asked to come off their line and collect the crosses if they felt they could do it successfully.

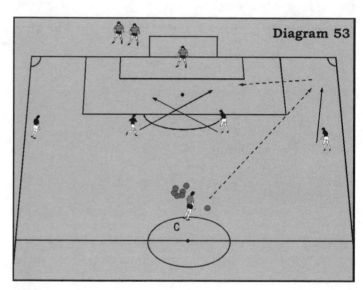

Diagram 53

Diagram 54

Soccer Volleyball

Playing 2 v 2, a knee high net was placed in the center of a 10 x 5-yard area. The game was played like volleyball except the players used their heads and feet. The objective was to get the ball over the net and into the opponent's half with a maximum of three passes while keeping the ball in the air. The ball was allowed to hit the ground once during the three passes.

Coaching Young Players

Contributed by the Challenger Sports, British Soccer coaching staff. Challenger Sports is a nationwide provider of camps and clinics. Challenger conducts over 1200 "BRITISH SOCCER CAMPS", coaching over 55,000 players and 10,000 coaches in 48 states. The following practices are part of Challenger's "Learning Through Games" curriculum aimed at players 6-9 years old. For further information, visit their web site at www.challengersports.com

Unopposed Dribbling - Captain On Deck

Organization: In a 15 x 15-yard area, each player has a ball and dribbles around inside the grid. The captain gives instructions that the players follow: Fast - Slow - Turn - Stop - Left foot - Right foot - Port - Starboard - Stern - Bow etc.

Development

Players get to experiment with their own twists, turns and stops.

Coaching Points

No walking, keep the ball moving, keep the ball within playing distance.

Feedback

"Can you use lots of little touches to keep the ball close?"

"How can you stop yourself from falling over the ball when you stop suddenly?"

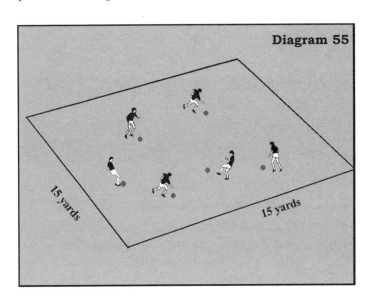

Diagram 55

15 yards

15 yards

Opposed Dribbling - Stuck in the Mud

Organization: In a 20 x 20-yard area, each player has a ball apart from two players who are the defenders. The players dribble their balls inside the grid and try to avoid the two defenders who have to try and tag them. If they get tagged, they are "stuck in the mud" and they hold their soccer balls above their heads with their legs apart. The only way they can get out of the mud is by having one of the dribblers pass their ball through their legs. Can the defenders tag all of the attackers?

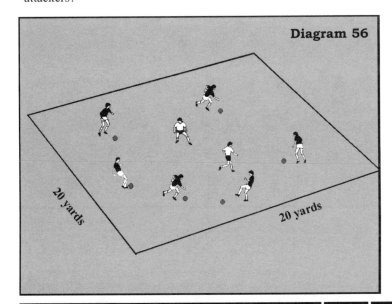

Diagram 56

20 yards

20 yards

Development

Increase the number of defenders.

Coaching Points

Close control, keeping the ball moving, head up to locate defender, use outside & inside of foot to dribble, use of variety of turns.

Feedback

"Can you use at least two different turns?"

"Try to find someone stuck in the mud"

"Can we push the ball out in front of us?"

"Remember to keep your head up!"

Dribbling Game - Pokemon Crab Attack

Organization: In a 25 x 20-yard area, each player has a ball and attempts to dribble past "Crabby" to get to the sea. If Crabby can take away the soccer ball from the dribblers, the dribbler is caught and joins crabby for the next round making two Crabbies. The dribblers continue until there is only one left.

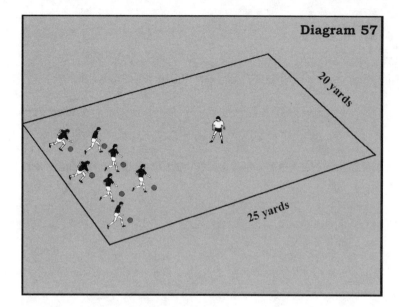

Diagram 57

20 yards

25 yards

Development
Crabby evolves into Bulbasor (hops) and then into a Slow-Poke (can only walk).

Coaching Points
Use of outside and inside of foot to cut the ball from side to side to avoid the crab.

Feedback
"Remember to keep looking up for crabs"
"Can you slow down and then speed up to fool the crab?"

Unopposed Passing - Please And Thank You

Organization: In a 15 x 20-yard area, four players stand on each side of the grid. The players in the middle dribble around looking for free outside players. When they see one they ask them - "do you want a pass?". If the receiver says, "yes please", they make the pass and then say, "thank you" when they get the return pass.

Development
When the side players receive the ball, they switch places with the passer.

Coaching Points
No walking, keep looking up for a free side player. Lock ankle, good contact and follow through.

Feedback
"Can you pass while you are moving?"
"Can you try passing from a little further away?"

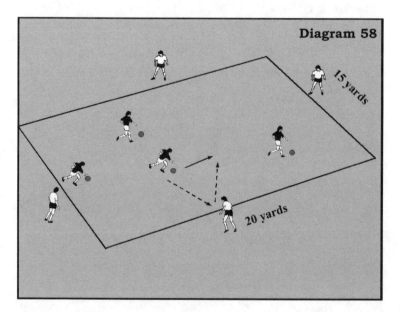

Diagram 58

15 yards

20 yards

Coaching Young Players

Opposed Passing - Twenty One

Organization: In a 15 x 20-yard area, four players with one ball attempt to score points by making passes to each other - one point for each pass made correctly. As soon as they make a pass, they have to go and "re-energize" by running around one of the six cones. The lone defender scores three points for each time that he touches the ball. Scoring is continuous and the first to 21 points wins.

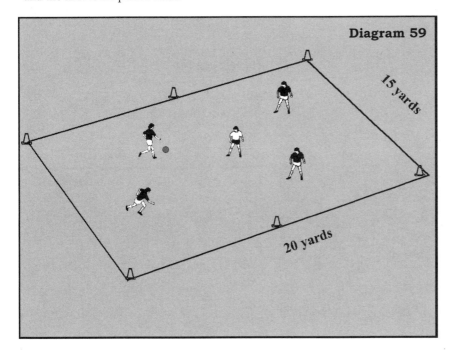

Diagram 59

15 yards

20 yards

Development
Add a second defender.

Coaching Points
Angle of pass, timing and strength.

Feedback
"Can you control the ball in the direction of where you will make your next pass?"
"Can you try passing with your other foot?"

Passing Game - Zone Passing

Organization: In a 25 x 20-yard area, play 3 v 3. Each team attempts to score points by making a pass to one of their own players in the end zone (third of field) and then for every consecutive pass made in that zone. If the ball gets kicked out, the other team has an unopposed pass into play.

Development
Have goals on each end-line. As soon as you score in one goal, you switch and begin attacking the other goal.

Coaching Points
Create angles, support the player with the ball, go backwards to get away from pressure.

Feedback
"Can you show your teammate where you want the pass?"
"Can you move as soon as you have passed it to help your team mate?"

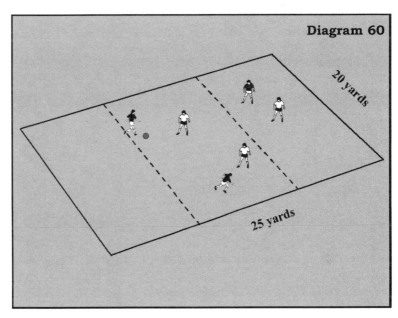

Diagram 60

20 yards

25 yards

Coaching Young Players

Unopposed Turning - Turnaround

Organization: In a 20 x 20-yard area with one ball per player and 12 flat cones placed around the perimeter, the players run around with their ball. On command, they have to dribble to an outside cone and score a point if they can turn without touching the cone with their ball. Play for 30 seconds, how many points can you score? Repeat trying to beat your own score.

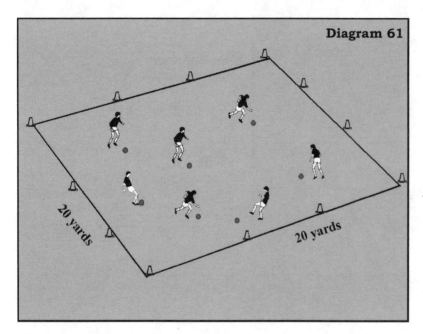

Diagram 61

20 yards

20 yards

Development

Increase the size of the area and vary the position of the cones. The coach also now adds "turn" on his command at any point in the grid.

Coaching Points

Use of different turns (e.g. inside, outside), technique of the turns, speed before and after cones, head up to locate the free cones.

Feedback

"Why did you touch the cone?"
"What happens if we go too fast?"
"Can you do different turns each time?"

Opposed Turning - Monster Turnaround

Organization: In a 20 x 20-yard area, organize one ball per player and two "Monsters" without a ball. The players run around with their ball. To score points they have to run towards a monster and execute a turn. They score a point if they can turn away from the monster keeping control of the ball. If they get too close, the monster can kick their ball away, which they then have to retrieve. How many points can you score in 30 seconds? Repeat trying to beat your own score.

Development

Only half of the dribblers have balls. They can now turn away from the monsters and then pass to a teammate to escape. The monster can intercept passes.

Coaching Points

Distance when turning, speed before and after a turn.

Feedback

"How can we protect the ball?"
"What speed do we need to approach the monster?"
"When should we pass and when should we turn?"

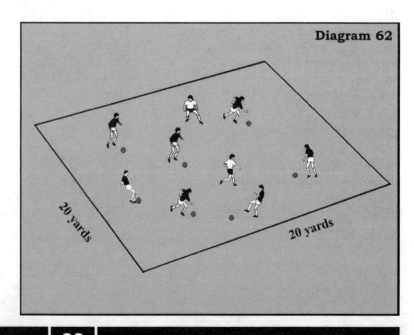

Diagram 62

20 yards

20 yards

Coaching Young Players

Turning Game - Four Goal Game

Organization: In a 25 x 25-yard area, divide the group into four teams. Two teams play on each field. Play a 4 v 4 small-sided game with the team in possession able to score in any one of the four goals. Goals can be scored by dribbling through from either side of the goal.

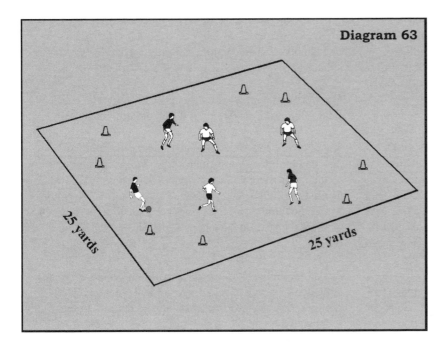

Diagram 63

25 yards

25 yards

Development

As above, but condition the game so that you can only score from one side. Goals can now only be scored by shooting.

Coaching Points

Turn away from a crowded area and attack a free goal. Find space to receive passes to score.

Feedback

"Can you see the goal - if not, which other goal can you see?"

"Show me a good position to receive a pass to score."

"Could we have had a shot with your (left or right) foot there?"

"Where is the space?" "How can we find space?"

Ajax - A System of Play

Contributed by subscriber, Alan Maher. Alan has coached at the college and high school level. He has written articles for the NSCAA Soccer Journal, Southern Soccer Scene and the New York Times. Alan has been visiting Holland for over 20 years and has observed the training sessions of many Dutch teams. This article is the result of observations of the system of play of the Ajax youth teams when Louis van Gaal was the head coach and Co Adriaanse was head of the youth programs.

A national soccer newspaper reported that Ajax played a 3-4-3 system of play. I can understand the confusion due to the fluid way that Ajax plays. The three lines are linked and it could be called a 3-4-3 system. However, a recent Dutch magazine interviewed Louis van Gaal, and in the article he said that Ajax played a system of 4-3-3.

As can be seen in diagram 32, the system of play looks like a series of interlocking diamonds. Actually, player #10 plays behind and to the right of player #9. But the overall impression is of a series of diamonds. So it looks like a 3-4-3 system but it is considered to be 4-3-3 by van Gaal and staff. I translated some comments in one article a few years ago and felt that I must verify what I read. Please consult diagram 32 and follow the response by Co Adriaanse who is in charge of youth training.

He wrote, "In each Ajax youth team, there are 16 players, four for positions 2-6-7, four for positions 5-8-11, three for positions 3-4, three for positions 9-10 and two for positions 1 (the goalkeeper)."

The players are grouped for training purposes a little differently than you would expect. They are trained in groups going up and down the field. Thus, players 5-8-11 work together as do 2-6-7 on the other side. Also, the outside players can combine with the players in the middle spine. Thus, players 6 or 8 combine with 4 and 10.

Of interest to me was not only the system of play, which is rather fluid to begin with, but the actual training system.

Traditionally coaches will train a line against a line or against two lines. For instance, a typical practice of six against four is combining the middle and forward lines against the defensive line. Be the system of play 4-3-3 or 4-4-2, the middle and front lines combine to make a group of six players while the defensive line is the remaining four players.

Ajax does things a little differently. They would combine defender #5 with midfield player #8 and wing #11. That changes the complexion of training and the way of even looking at a team and its sub-groups. For me it was an eye opener. The thrust of the training sessions is always to advance the ball when the groups are formed that way.

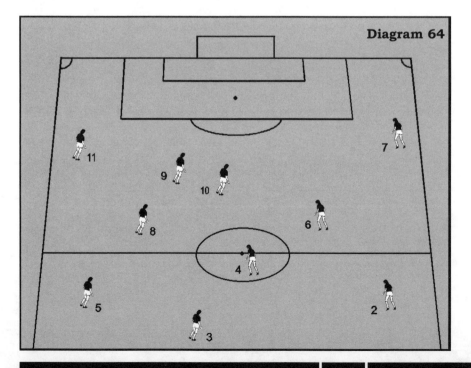

Diagram 64

Ajax - Playing Formation

Liverpool F.C.

This practice conducted by assistant manager and first team coach Sammy Lee was observed in October 2000. Liverpool had just played a game the day before against Derby County in the English Premier League and this practice consisted of the players from the first team squad that hadn't played in that game. This group of players were also due to play a "Friendly" game against a local non-league team that same evening so the practice was rather light.

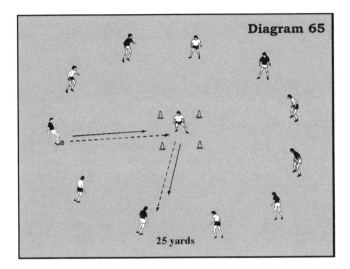

Diagram 65

25 yards

Circle Warm-Up

After 10 minutes of jogging and stretching, the 12 players were organized into two teams of six and formed a 20-yard circle with cones marking a 3-yard square in the center as shown in diagram 65. Start with one player in the center. Using one ball, pass to the player in the center square who controls with one touch and passes to a player of the opposite team with the second touch. Each player follows his pass.

Coaching Points

- Fill the gaps on the perimeter of the circle as they appear by adjusting your position
- Quality of passes and controlling touch
- Angles

Progression

Now have two players in the center. The ball is passed in to player A who lays it off with one touch to player B. Player B passes to a perimeter player of the opposite team. The pass to the center player can be to either of the two players regardless of which team they are on.

Coaching Points

- Inside players have one touch, perimeter players have two touches
- Communicate - let them know if you are passing to them
- Progress to one-touch for everyone

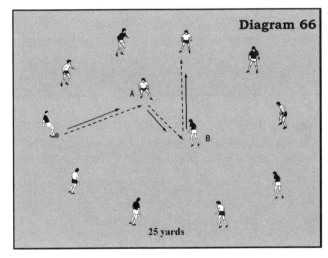

Diagram 66

A

B

25 yards

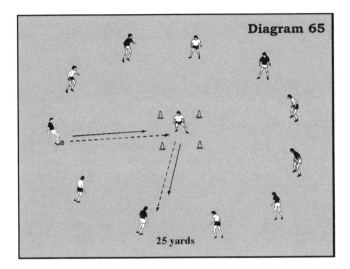

Diagram 67

20 yards

25 yards

Throw-Head-Volley

Use full size goals on a 25 x 20-yard area. The ball is passed by throwing it to a teammate who volleys or heads the ball to another teammate or for a shot on goal. Attempt to build up play with passing and moving rather than by throwing long passes.

Note: The total practice was 60 minutes long.

Liverpool F.C. U17 & U19

This practice was conducted by Steve Heighway, the Director of the Liverpool Youth Academy and the U17 and U19 youth team coaches, Dave Shannon and Hugh McCauley. There were a total of 21 players from the two teams. This practice followed a long weekend break for the players with no games, so an element of conditioning was involved.

Warm-Up

Following a one-mile run and a series of stretches, the players were split into three groups of seven. Each group worked at a different station for four minutes followed by two minutes of stretches.

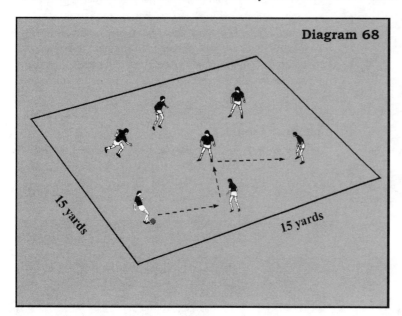

Diagram 68

Station One

In a 15 x 15-yard square, using one ball, the players passed and moved using only one-touch. First they tried to spread out making as much space as possible to pass into, then for the last minute or so they got closer together and did quick short passes.

Coaching Points

- Move away as soon as you have made a pass
- Ask for a quick return pass
- Receive with an open body position
- Communicate

Station Two

The same as Station One except the players must use two touches.

Coaching Points

- A soft receiving touch to one side followed by a firm pass
- Use all surfaces to pass and receive
- Use both feet

Station Three

A series of cones are positioned 10-yards apart as shown in diagram 69. The players are grouped to start simultaneously at each end and do a series of runs between the cones.

Runs

- Side-to-side
- Jump for headers between each cone
- Side leg raises
- Defensive jockeying posture

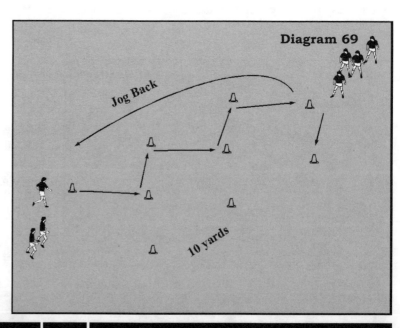

Diagram 69

Jog Back

10 yards

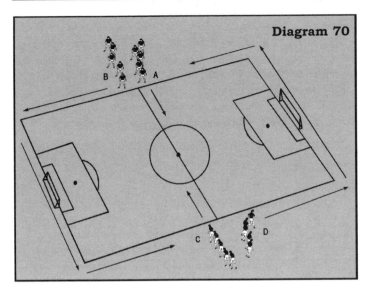

Diagram 70

Conditioning

The players line up in four groups at the half-line as shown in diagram 70. Groups B and D sprint at 75% pace around 3/4 of half a field to the half line on the other side. Groups A and C jog slowly across the field to the other side of the half line. The timing should be so that all the groups arrive at the opposite end of the half line at the same time. Then groups B and D jog slowly across the field and A and C sprint around the field. Each group did a total of six sprints and jogs.

Half-Field Game

Play 11 v 11 across a half-field. The offside rule is in effect only over the lines that are marked 15 yards from goal. Play two 15-minute halves.

Observations

The game was played at a quick pace and was very competitive. The coaches stopped play only a few times and were very quick and firm with their coaching points.

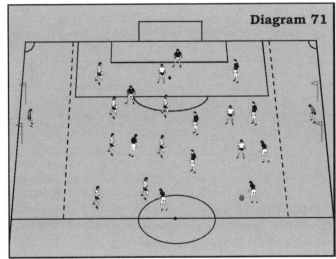

Diagram 71

Nepal National Team

Contributed by Stephen Constantine, Head Coach of the Nepal National Team. Stephen is a holder of both the USSF and UEFA 'A' Licenses. After three years coaching in the U.S., Stephen, a native of England, moved to Cyprus where he coached at professional clubs Ahilleas F.C., Ael F.C. and Apep F.C. of the Cyprus First Division, where he was the head coach. In July 1998 Constantine was invited to join the England Under 18 National Team coaching staff at the UEFA Championships where England qualified for the World Cup in Nigeria with responsibilities for scouting. In August 1999 he was appointed head coach of the Nepal National Team. The following training session can be used to focus on defending, attacking, conditioning or technical work. This article is focused on the defending aspect.

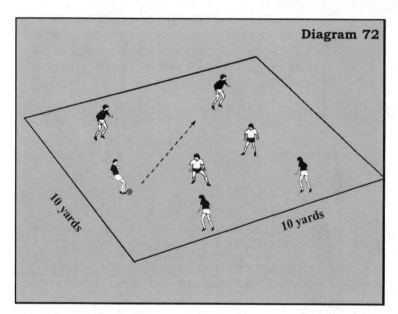

Diagram 72

Warm-Up

Organize the players into groups of seven and play 5 v 2 keepaway in a 10 x 10-yard area. Play for 10 - 15 minutes. Stretch before, during and after the exercise. Each pair of defenders work for 60 - 90 seconds.

Coaching Points

- Coach the two defenders
- Defend as a pair - the closest defender applies the pressure, the second defender provides support
- Don't get split by a pass
- The pressurizing defender attempts to force the pass in one direction - this shows the covering defender where to provide the cover

Warm-Up

Diagram 73 shows the correct position for the pressurizing defender and the covering defender. The pressurizing defender is in a position that is forcing the player with the ball to pass in only one direction. The covering defender is in a position to intercept the ball if it is passed to player B or both defenders would be in a good position to box in player A if the ball is passed to him.

Coaching Points

- The covering defender should be aware that the ball can only be passed in one direction
- Communicate

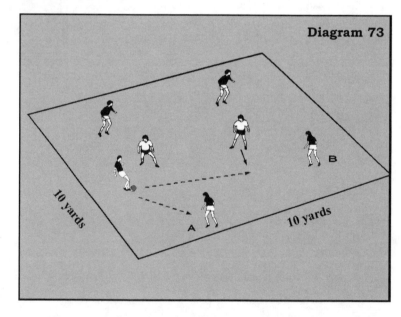

Diagram 73

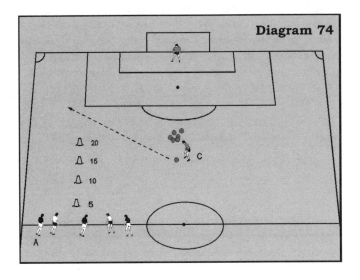

Diagram 74

Doggies - Defending

Organize the players into groups of 3 v 2 on the half-line as shown in diagram 74. Place four cones five yards apart in a line extending toward the goal-line. Together the players sprint to each cone and back. On the final sprint to the 20-yard cone, the coach passes a ball into the path of the widest attacking player, player A who crosses into the penalty area. The other two attackers run into the goalbox to get on the end of the cross. The two defenders try to defend the cross. Alternate the players to allow adequate rest time.

Coaching Points

- Try to block the cross
- Defend the near post area
- Get your body position across and in front of the incoming forward

Transition Defending

The two "A" players attack the lone defender. Once the attack is completed, the three "B" players start to attack and the two "A" players defend, creating a 3 v 2 situation. As soon as that attack has ended, the four "C" players start their attack and are defended by the three "B" players making a 4 v 3 situation. This is followed by the five "D" players in a 5 v 4 situation against the four "C" players. After defending, the players jog back to the half-line.

Coaching Points

- Quick transition from offense to defense as soon as the attack is completed
- Pressure the player with the ball quickly

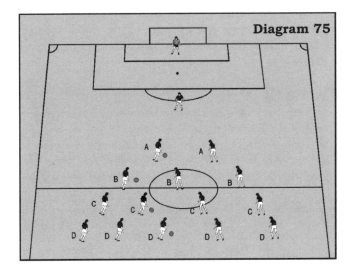

Diagram 75

Barnsley F.C.

Contributed by long-time subscriber Gerry Canavan. Ten years ago at the age of 15 Gerry spent the summer training with Sheffield United, then in the English Premier League. At the time, Dave Bassett was the manager of Sheffield United. Over the last 10 years Gerry has been fortunate to visit Bassett as his coaching career has taken him to Nottingham Forest and now, Barnsley F.C. of the English First Division. In 2000, Gerry spent six weeks at Barnsley F.C. observing practices of all the teams and even training with the youth and reserve teams as well as helping to coach the younger Academy players. Gerry also traveled with the players and coaching staff as he observed the games of the first team, reserves and youth teams. Gerry is an active coach (USSF "B" License and NSCAA Advanced Diploma) in his home town of Chicago where he is Director of Coaching for the Wilmette Wings S.C.

Gerry would like to thank Barnsley F.C., Dave Bassett, John Greaves, Derek French and all of the coaching staff and players for their hospitality and kindness over his six-week stay.

Monday

Practice begins promptly at 10.00 am with Assistant Manager, Peter Shirtliff. The Barnsley first team players rested on Sunday following their Saturday game against Queens Park Rangers. The primary focus of Monday's training session is to have all the first team players recover from the game: this means injured players receive treatment, and all the healthy players will have an easy day of training. The players that did not play in Saturday's match will train with the first team but will participate in extra running at the end of training with the youth team players. Usually these players would train with the reserves, but the reserve team is playing tonight against Liverpool F.C.'s reserve team. The reserves will have a light session and rehearse set pieces such as free kicks, and corner kicks. The goalkeepers always train with the goalkeeper coach, Andy Rhodes, for the first half of practice, and then join the rest of the team for game situation exercises or scrimmages. Today there will be no full-sided game so the goalkeepers will remain with their coach for all of the session.

Warm-Up

Assistant manager Peter Shirtliff leads the first team players on a jog and stretch routine. The players jog up and down the field, periodically stretching. After each stretch the intensity gradually increases. About half way through the warm-up, the players perform a series of strideouts across the width of the field. The players are not allowed to sprint to start with and can only run at a 75% maximal effort during the strideouts. The strideouts then progress into more jogging, some sprinting, and even more stretching. The warm-up lasts about 20 minutes.

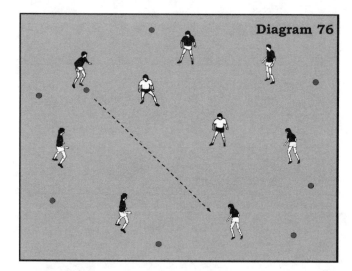

Diagram 76

Circle Work - Keep-Away

The players are organized into groups of nine with seven perimeter players playing keep-away from two defenders in a small 6 - 8-yard circle. The player responsible for losing possession switches position with the defender. Play for 15 minutes. Start with two-touch and progress to one-touch. Keep a supply of balls outside the circle to keep the game flowing.

Coaching Points

- Good first touch
- Quick passing and decisions
- Make it fun

Observations

Although this is typically a fun warm-up game for a Monday, the players worked hard and exhibited good technique and awareness in such a tight space, while being pressured from the middle players. Even in the smallest of areas the ball is flicked, back-heeled and even lifted over the two defenders in the middle. The players were laughing, joking, and having playful banter amongst each other, especially when mistakes were made and a new player must enter the middle.

Barnsley F.C.

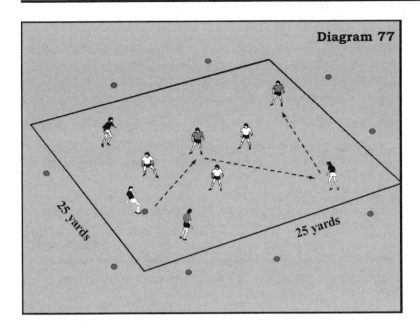

Diagram 77

3 v 3 v 3 Keep-Away

Organize three teams of three players in a 25 x 25-yard area. Each team has a different colored jersey. Two teams combine to play 6 v 3 keep-away against the other three players. The team that is responsible for losing possession becomes the defending team. Play for 25 minutes starting with three-touch, progressing to two-touch and then one-touch. Have a supply of balls around the perimeter to keep the game flowing.

Coaching Points
- Body shape should change in relation to the ball's movement.
- Good passing and receiving technique
- Work hard - chase to get the ball back

Observations
The coaching points reinforced by coach Shirtliff might appear basic on the surface; however, his intensity and enthusiasm radiated from the players throughout the exercise. Although this was a simple possession game, the speed, technical excellence, athleticism, and quickness-of-thought made the passing exercise far from basic. What impressed me the most was the emphasis on working hard to get the ball back, and when the players won it they took pride not only in keeping it, but also in punishing the other three players when they lost the ball. I could not help admire the quality of the players' first touch, and their ability to make decisions in milli-seconds. Especially, Craig Hignett who made numerous little flicks and fakes that split defenders in the tightest of spaces, while never giving away possession of the ball.

Warm-Down
Training ends with all of the first team players going on a 20-minute jog/run with the Assistant Manager, Pete Shirtliff. The players leave the training ground and jog along a countryside path for about two miles with plenty of stretching along the way. Shirtliff's objective is to remove any remaining lactic acid in the player's muscles from the weekend, while maintaining flexibility and fitness. The players who did not play on Sunday participated in an interval running circuit with the youth team at the end of training. This included brisk walking, jogging, and sprinting. The reserve team wrapped-up their set pieces for that night, and ended training early. After the running circuit, the remaining first team players jogged and stretched for 10 minutes.

Monday Evening 7.00 pm - Barnsley Reserves v Liverpool Reserves
I traveled on the team bus to watch the reserve game against Liverpool F.C., which is the team I grew up supporting. Over 4,000 Liverpool fans showed up at the St. Helen's Rugby Ground for a 7.00 p.m. kickoff. Gerard Houllier, the Liverpool Manager fielded a strong team, because they did not have a league game scheduled for almost three weeks. The captain, Sami Hypia, Titi Camara, Domenic Matteo, and Stig Bjornebye are a few of the well-known first team players that play throughout the match. Barnsley fields a young reserve team made up primarily of U-19 Academy players.

Barnsley F.C.

Game Tactics

The Reserve Team coach Marc Smith informed me that he would attempt to play with a screen player in front of the back four. He would also ask the outside midfield players to position themselves tighter to the center midfielder in order to brake up any service to the forwards, and to prevent any passing through Barnsley's midfield. This seems like a logical tactic, because Liverpool is a highly skilled team who has a history of carving open an opposing team's midfield with their precise and methodical passing.

Barnsley is effective for most of the first half; however, Liverpool scores its first goal when their right fullback bypasses the midfield with a long diagonal ball to Titi Camara on the left side of the field, who holds off a challenge from the right fullback and then beats the keeper 1 v 1. Unfortunately, Barnsley's tactics were foiled by Liverpool's high level of skill, strength, and execution. The young Barnsley squad never stopped working hard and created a handful of chances, but was unable to make the best of their opportunities. The Barnsley team chased the game for most of the second half and lost to an experienced Liverpool side 0 - 3.

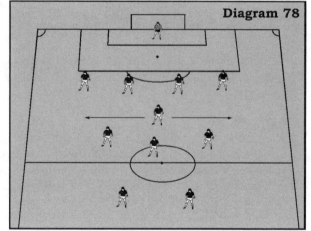

Diagram 78

The highlight of my evening was running out of the tunnel onto the field when the crowd sang their trademark song, "You'll Never Walk Alone", which always occurs a few minutes before the kickoff. Although I was a guest of Barnsley F.C, I could not help but "accidentally" stand behind the last member of Liverpool's staff when they ran out of the tunnel. I fulfilled a childhood dream by running out onto the pitch with Liverpool F.C. Two of Barnsley's staff, John Greaves and Derek French gave me a hard time when they turned around and saw me applauding and waving to the crowd, as if I were a player. Then to top off the memorable moment, I sat on the Barnsley bench throughout the match, listened to the half time talk, and traveled home on the team bus. What an experience!

L.A. Galaxy

This was a pre-season practice observed in February 2000. At this time the MLS teams were practicing twice a day which included some scrimmages against other teams and games in the MLS pre-season tournament.

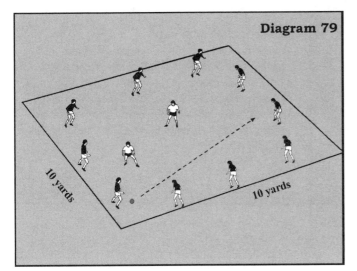

Diagram 79

Warm-Up

The players were organized into two groups of 12 and each group played 10 v 2 keep-away in a 10 x 10-yard area. The players started off with two-touch for the first five minutes and progressed to one-touch for the last five minutes.

This was followed by 15 minutes of jogging and stretching.

Technical Warm-Up

Organize the players into groups of three, each group in a 10 x 10-yard area. Player A and B each have a ball and take turns passing the ball to player C who moves side-to-side to receive the passes and return them back. Play for one minute and then rotate so that each player has a turn receiving passes. Once the rotation is complete, stretch for two minutes.

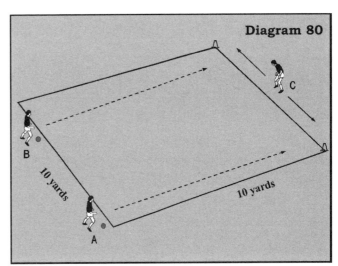

Diagram 80

Diagram 81

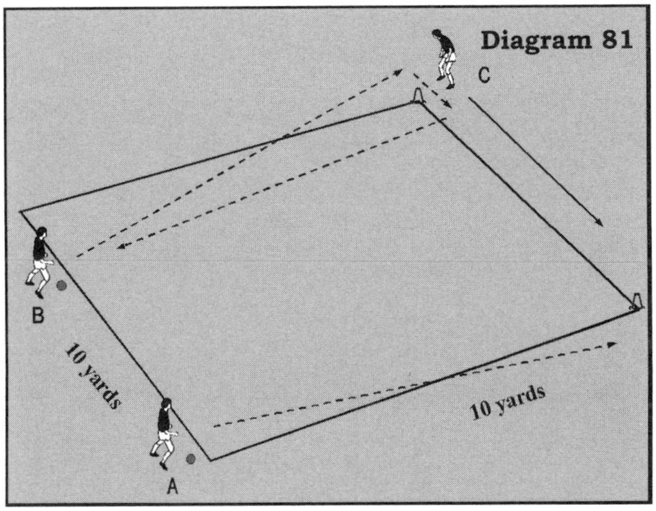

Technical Warm-Up

Use the same organization as in diagram 80, except this time players A and B pass the ball outside the cone. Player C controls the ball to the inside of the cone with one foot and passes back with the other foot. Play for one minute and then rotate so that each player has a turn receiving passes. Once the rotation is complete, stretch for two minutes.

L.A. Galaxy

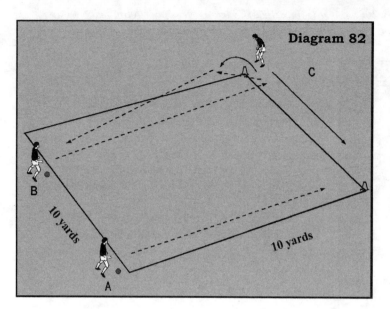

Diagram 82

Technical Warm-Up

Again use the same organization as diagram 80, except this time pass the ball inside the cones. Player C controls the ball in front of and outside of the cone and passes back. Play for one minute and then rotate so that each player has a turn receiving passes. Once the rotation is complete, stretch for two minutes.

Practice ended with an 11 v 11 game on a full field of two 25-minute halves.

Coaching Young Players

Contributed by Julian Owen, Arkansas State Soccer Association - Director of Coaching and Player Development. Julian holds the F.A. of Wales Senior Coaching License and the USSF National Youth License. Prior to his coaching career Julian played professional soccer in his home country for Swansea City F.C. The following sessions focus on technical training for youth players.

Fundamental Stage - Receiving

Organize the players in pairs 30 - 40 yards apart as shown in diagram 83. The players pass to each other using various techniques - high, low, driven, lofted passes, etc.

The players receive the ball with different surfaces - inside of foot, outside of foot, thigh, chest, etc.

If needed the players could also get closer and throw the ball to their partner to make sure they are getting lots of repetitions receiving air balls.

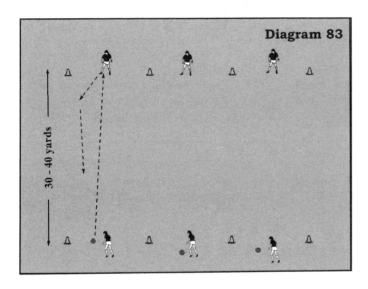

Diagram 83

30 - 40 yards

Coaching Points

- Get in line with the flight of the ball
- Early decision on which surface to use
- Keep your eyes on the ball
- Move towards the ball
- With your first touch try and change the direction of the ball and play it back without the ball stopping
- With your first touch get the ball out of your feet so you will have time to look at the target

Game Related Stage - Receiving

Organize six players inside a 35-yard area and six players on the perimeter. The players on the outside have a ball each. The players on the outside pass the ball to the players on the inside. The inside players control the ball, pass it back then move to receive another ball from a different player.

Progression

- The inside players control the ball on the turn and play it to a different outside player
- The outside players serve the ball by hand for the inside players to chest control or thigh control
- Add a defender or two to try and win the ball inside the area

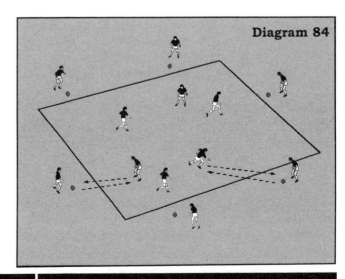

Diagram 84

Coaching Young Players

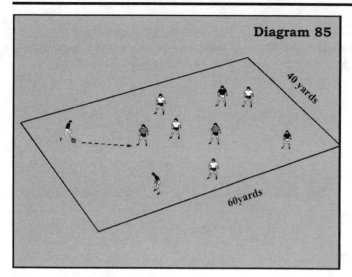

Diagram 85

Game Condition Stage - Receiving

Organize 4 v 4 plus two neutral players who play for the team in possession. Play keep-away. Points are awarded for a pre-determined number of consecutive passes. Every second pass must be over 15 yards long.

Progressions

- Limit touches - two touches, etc.
- Add goals

Coaching Points

- First touch away from pressure
- Keep the ball moving with your first touch
- Position of your body - open body to face the field

Fundamental Stage - Dribbling

Organize four markers set up in diamond fashion 10 to 15 yards from the grid. The size of the grid would depend on the number and age of the players. Each player dribbles his or her ball inside the grid. The players use different dribbling techniques - left foot only, right foot only, inside and outside of foot, etc. and also change directions on the coaches signal.

Progression

- The players dribbling while trying to tag other players with their hand. Any player tagged must leave his ball and sprint around an outside marker then the player may join back in.
- Instead of tagging, the players try to knock other players' balls out of the grid. The players that lose their ball must sprint around the marker with their ball before they can join back in.

Coaching Points

Change pace, get into open space, head up, awareness

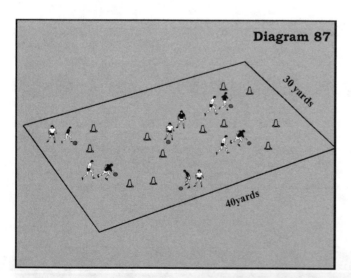

Diagram 87

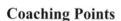

Diagram 86

Game Related Stage - Dribbling

Play 1 v 1 inside a 40 x 30-yard grid with six randomly placed goals marked by cones as shown in diagram 40. The objective is to score a goal by dribbling through any of the goals. If the defender wins the ball, he attempts to score. This game is hard work for about 60 seconds then rest in between.

Coaching Point

Fake towards one goal then go to another.

Game Condition Stage - Dribbling

Organize two teams of three players. Each team should have a goalkeeper, a defender and a forward. The defenders must stay in the defensive half and the forwards must stay in the attacking half. Play starts with the goalkeeper who throws the ball to the forward in the opposite half. When the forward receives the ball he should try and turn, then dribble into a shooting position. If the defender wins the ball he tries to get it to his attacker. Use a dribble-in if the ball goes out of play.

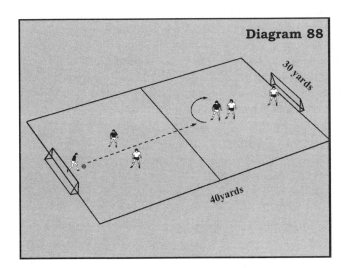

Diagram 88

30 yards

40yards

Progression

Play 5 v 5, two forwards in each zone and two defenders in each zone plus a goalkeeper.

Coaching Points

- Turn on the defender by checking off the defender
- Control the pass on the half turn
- Dribble at the defender, fake one way and accelerate the other way
- Eyes slightly ahead so you can see ball and the defender

Leeds United U17 Youth Team

Contributed by Warren Joyce, Leeds United U17 youth team coach. These practices are technical/tactical sessions that can be used as a warm-up focusing on passing, receiving and movement.

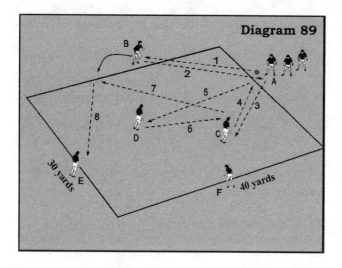

Warm-Up One

After 10 minutes of jogging and stretching, the players are organized as in diagram 89. Player A passes to player B. Player B passes straight back to player A who then passes to player C. Player C passes back to player A who then passes to player D. Player D lays the ball off to player C who passes to player B. Player B passes to player E. Player E then continues the drill using the other side by passing to player F. The outside players rotate positions in a clockwise direction and players C and D rotate positions.

Coaching Points

- Players C and D stay in the middle while the other players rotate anti-clockwise
- Quality of passes and controlling touch

Warm-Up Two

The players make slight adjustments to their positions as seen in diagram 90. Player A passes to player B who passes straight back to player A. Player A passes long to player D who lays the ball off for player C, who has spun around to receive the pass. Player C passes to player B. Player B passes to player E. Player E then continues the drill using the other side by passing to player F. The outside players rotate positions in a clockwise direction and players C and D rotate positions.

Coaching Points

- Inside players have one touch, perimeter players have two touches
- Progress to one-touch for everyone

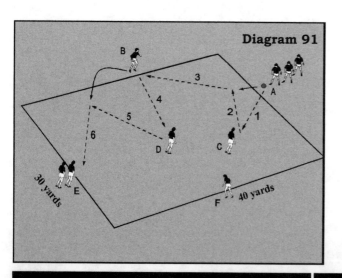

Warm-Up Three

The objective of this warm-up is to work the wide players and have them playing 'balls around the corner' to the front players and then support. Player A passes short to player C who lays the ball back to player A. Player A passes to player B who passes inside to player D. Player D passes into the path of running player B who passes to player E. Player E then continues the drill using the other side by passing to player F. The outside players rotate positions in a clockwise direction and players C and D rotate positions.

Coaching Points

- Wide player must check to the ball and play the pass with his outside foot
- Play two-touch to start then progress to one-touch

Leeds United U17 Youth Team

Progression To Small-Sided Game

The objective of the session is to work specifically on passing, receiving, movement off the ball, communication and finishing. The field is set up as shown in diagram 92 in a 40 x 35-yard area with four small goals or flags - two placed at the ends and two on the sides. The players are split into two teams of six. There are no goalkeepers and the team that scores a goal maintains possession.

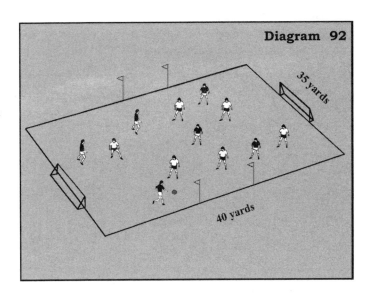

Diagram 92

Game One

Play 6 v 6. Following six passes, the team in possession may score in any of the four goals.

Progressions

- Score in any one of the four goals with no conditions
- Hit the back of the net without the ball bouncing
- Can only score with a one-touch finish

Game Two

The game is limited in time to three minutes. One team (dark team) is given possession and their task is to maintain possession for the three minutes. Should the other team gain possession, then they are limited to two-touch and four passes before they can score, with a one-touch finish, in any of the four goals. Following every goal, the dark team regains possession.

Repeat the game with the white team having possession and the dark team trying to score as many goals as possible within the three minutes. The team that scores the most goals in the three minutes wins.

Coaching Points

- The best way to stop the other team from scoring is to keep the ball for as long as possible within the three minutes.
- First touch, passing ability and movement off the ball are crucial to the success of keeping possession
- Encourage good habits of communication

General Coaching Points For Game One and Two

- Passing awareness - encourage the players to 'have something in mind' before they receive the ball
- Encourage as many 'give-and-go's' as possible in order to achieve a better position to pass again or to shoot
- Man-for-man Marking - highlight staying with the runners and to 'switch on' as soon as possession is lost
- Communication - highlight the importance of good communication in terms of who matches up with who

Depending on your theme and focus, you can get several sessions from this basic organization.

Coaching Young Players

Contributed by Wayne Harrison. Wayne is the holder of the EUFA "A" License and played and coached at the professional level in England prior to his current position of Director of Coaching and Player Development for Eden Prairie Soccer Club in Minnesota. This article is a series of small-sided games designed to teach young players the skills and techniques for dribbling.

Warm Up

Each player is given a ball as seen in diagram 93. The practice starts with each player dribbling and turning between each other. Slowly to begin with, then gradually spreading out, using the whole area. The coach acts as a passive defender and stops the practice regularly to allow the players to stretch.

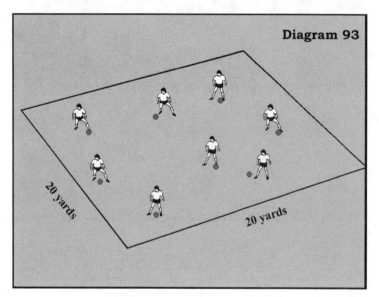

Coaching Points/Commands

- "Stop" - The players stand still with their foot on the ball
- "Change" - The players stop their own ball and go to someone else's ball and continue to dribble
- "Turn" - The players must change direction

Game One

Pick two players to act as defenders. All the other players each have a ball and must dribble continuously while protecting their ball. The defenders try to kick all the balls out of the area until there are no players dribbling. Each player takes his turn at being a defender.

Game Two

The players each have a ball and must protect their own ball while trying to kick someone else's ball out of the area. When your ball is kicked out, you can't kick another ball out.

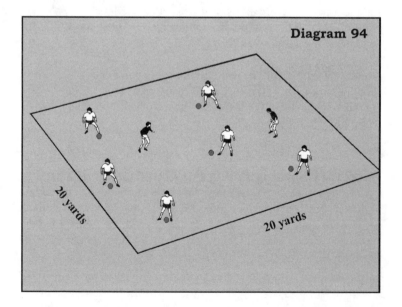

Coaching Young Players

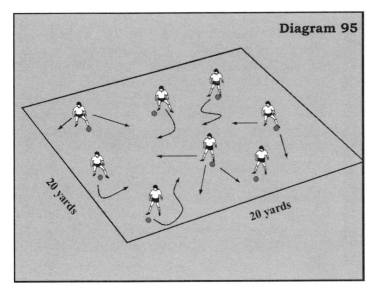

Diagram 95

Principles of Dribbling

Each player has a ball and dribbles and turns in a tight area avoiding other players. The coach dictates which techniques are to be practiced. This warm-up session concentrates on ball control with the quickening of movement.

Coaching Points

- Left or right foot turning (different types) only
- Changing pace
- Change soccer balls
- Check to the line and back into space

Shadow Dribbling

The players are paired off with a ball each. One player has to shadow the other, making the same movements. The lead player must try to lose their shadows while the shadows try to touch the leader. Rotate positions after two minutes.

Coaching Points

- Dribble with the outside of the foot only, inside only, left foot only and right foot only
- Turn and face your shadow and try to dummy them to try to get away

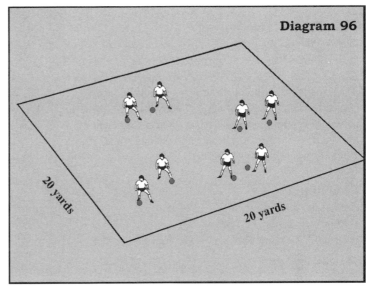

Diagram 96

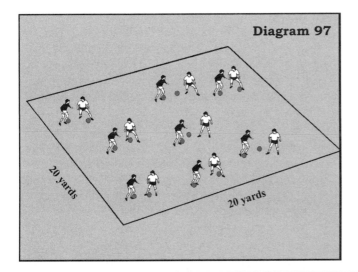

Diagram 97

Shadow Dribbling: Pairs

The practice progresses to include all 16 players at once. The congestion causes players to not only watch their leader more intently, but also to be aware of where other players are. (This should improve the players peripheral vision).

Kick-Out Game

Introduce the kick-out game for some fun. The players keep possession of their own ball while trying to kick someone else's out of the area. Once the player is out of the game, he must juggle with the ball to keep involved in some practice.

Coaching Young Players

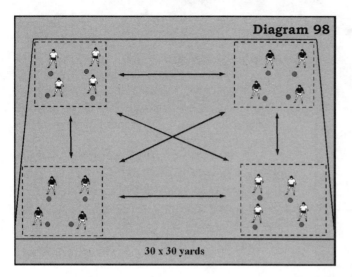

Diagram 98

30 x 30 yards

Dribbling And Running With The Ball

The players are split into four groups, each group in a 10 x 10-yard area practicing their designated dribbling moves and turns. On the command of the coach, they dribble as fast as they can to another grid, avoiding other players. The coach can determine the cut with the outside of the foot, the inside of the foot, full turn away from pressure, dummy step over, drag back and turn or step over and take.

Variation

Four players only go at once and cut to another group. The other players continue to dribble in their group until its their turn.

Two-Team Game

In this practice, the white team players have a ball each and try to keep it away from any of the dark team players. The dark players try to win a ball and keep it. (A player can win a ball off any of the other team's players). Once the player has lost possession of his ball, he must regain possession from another player. After a limited time period, the coach stops the game and sees which team has the most soccer balls.

Coaching Points

• Practice shielding the ball
• Improve peripheral vision
• Dribble and work with speed and strength

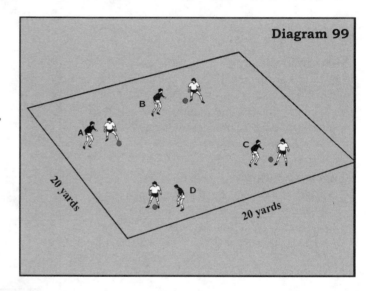

Diagram 99

20 yards

20 yards

Diagram 100

20 yards

20 yards

1 v 1's

Place 10 coned goals randomly inside the area. This is an intensive workout where each player must try to keep possession of the ball, and at the same time, score by dribbling through a goal. The players work for two minutes and count the number of goals they score through the various goals

Conditions

• Each player tries to gain possession of their partner's ball only
• Half the group goes first and once their time is up, they get a chance to recover and switch partners while the other half of the group goes

Humber College - Canada

Contributed by Germain Sanchez, Head Coach at Humber College. Humber College has won four outdoor and four indoor Provincial Championships during Sanchez's nine-year reign. They also won the National Championship in the 1995-1996 season. This session concentrates on conditioning drills with the ball for players of all levels and abilities.

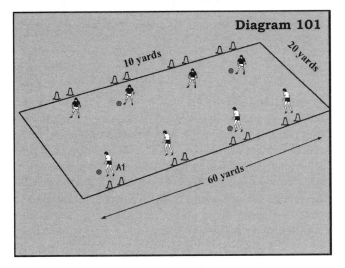

The Rotating Game

The players are organized in pairs across a 60 x 20-yard field. Each player defends his own small coned goal. Each player plays the opposite player in a one v one game. Each game is one minute long followed by a one-minute break.

Observations

During this conditioning game, players have to work on their dribbling and attacking skills when in possession and on their defensive skills, such as tackling, positioning and timing when not.

Development

After one minute of play, the coach stops the game, the balls go to the center and every player, except A1, rotates one space/field to their right. A1 remains, thus ensuring that nobody plays the same player twice.

Coaching Point

- Apply all defensive and attacking principles
- Play hard, but smart
- Use speed when the other player is tired

Note: Both these games are played with no lines or boundaries.

Progression

In this drill, the group is divided into pairs with each pair starting behind their goal. The small coned goals are now placed 40 yards apart. At the coaches command, player A1 plays player B1 from the opposite side while A2 and B2 wait behind their goals.

When one player scores, they stay on the field and the player waiting behind that goal immediately becomes an attacker. The player that was scored on goes behind that goal until another goal is scored in that goal.

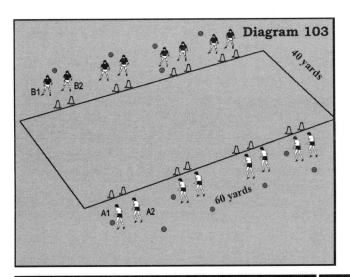

Ajax U17 Youth Team

Contributed by subscriber, Terry Michler. Terry has been the coach at Christian Brothers College High School, Saint Louis, MO for 30 years and has amassed a 602-159-74 record that includes 20 District Championships, nine State Final appearances and three State Championships. 230 of his former players have played college soccer and 32 have played professional soccer. Terry recently went on a 10-day trip to the Netherlands where he observed the training sessions of the Ajax professional and youth teams. This session is a series of passing drills conducted by the Ajax U17 team. Further sessions will appear in upcoming issues.

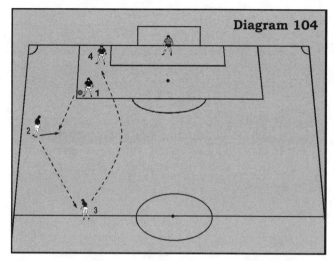

Passing Drill #1

Organize the players in a half-field as shown in diagram 104. This and the following exercises help the players become familiar with passing combinations designed to get the ball into goalscoring situations. Player 1 plays the ball up to player 2 who has checked away, then receives the ball sideways on before playing a pass to player 3. Player 3 can either play a long ball into player 4, dribble the ball back or play a long ball into the goalkeeper.

Passing Drill #2

Using the same set up as diagram 104, player 1 plays the ball up to player 2 who makes a flat, checked run before laying it back to player 1. Player 1 then plays a pass to player 3 who again, either plays a long pass to player 4, dribbles back or plays a long pass into the goalkeeper.

Passing Drill #3

Again using the same set up as in diagram 104, player 1 plays the pass up to player 2 who receives it sideways on. Player 2 turns and plays a pass up to player 3. Player 3 then plays a give-and-go with player 2 before setting himself up for a long range shot to finish.

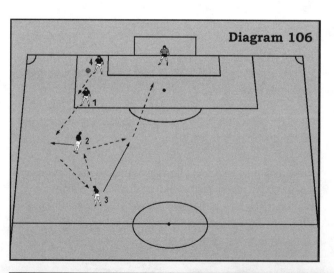

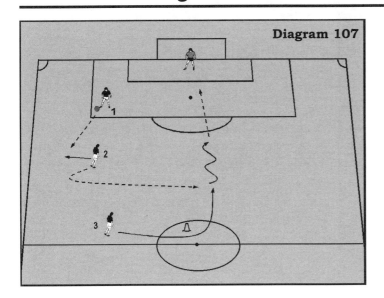

Diagram 107

Passing Drill #4

Player 2 makes a flat, checked run and receives a pass sideways on from player 1. Player 3 makes a timed run around the cone to receive a square pass from player 2. Player 3 then dribbles forward before shooting.

Passing Drill #5

Player 2 makes a flat, checked run and receives a pass sideways on from player 1 before laying it back. Player 1 then plays a long ball to player 3. Player 3 plays a give-and-go, around the cone, with player 2 before setting himself up for a shooting opportunity.

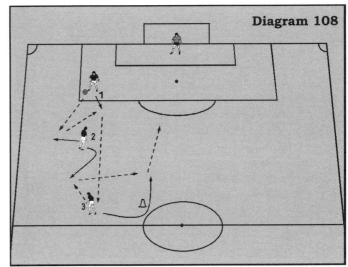

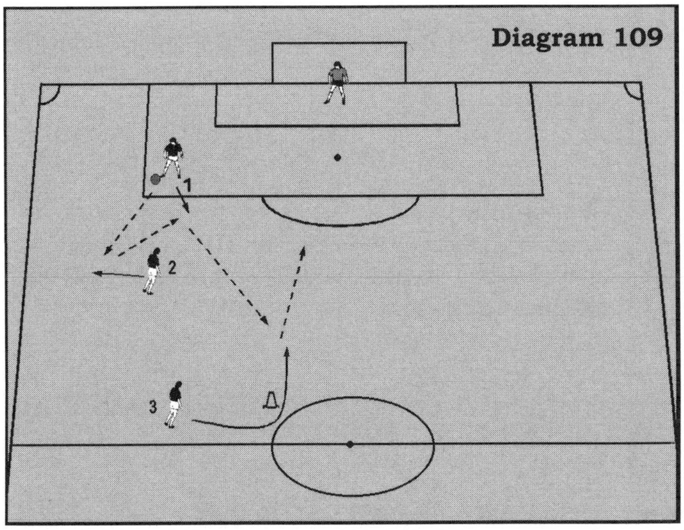

Diagram 108

Diagram 109

Passing Drill #6

Player 2 makes a flat, checked run and receives a pass sideways on from player 1 before laying it back. Player 1 then plays a long ball to player 3 who has made a timed run around a cone to receive the pass before running on to take a shot.

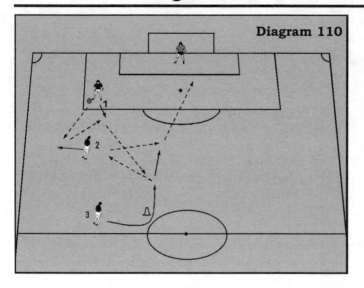

Diagram 110

Passing Drill #7

Player 1 plays a give-and-go with player 2 before playing a long ball to player 3. Player 3 has made a timed run around a cone to receive the long pass from player 1. Player 3 then plays a give-and-go with player 2, who has checked inside, and sets himself up for a long range shot.

Passing Drill #8

Use the same organization as the previous drills with the addition of a fourth player. Player 1 plays a give-and-go with player 2 before playing a long ball to player 3 who has made a timed run around a cone to receive it. Player 3 then plays a long diagonal pass to player 4 out on the wing. Player 3 makes a run to the far post and player 2 heads for the near post to receive a crossed ball by player 4.

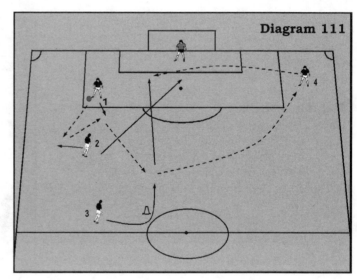

Diagram 111

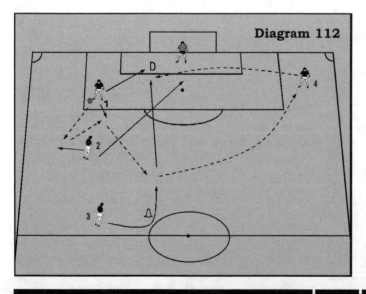

Diagram 112

Variation

Use the same set up as in diagram 111, however this time, player 1 becomes a defender once he initiates the passing sequence.

Chicago Fire

A pre-season training session with Bob Bradley and the Chicago Fire. As observed at Orlando, Florida, 2001

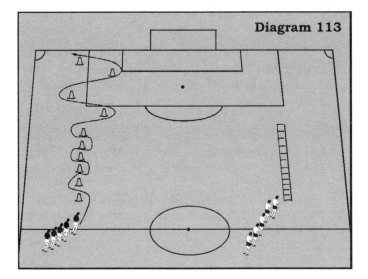

Warm Up

Coach Bob Bradley led the jogging around half a field while conducting several exercises: arm swinging, hopping, bounding, skipping, heel flicks, high knees, etc. The club trainer then led the stretching routine within a team circle. The coach then introduced poles or cones and ladders and led two separate groups through a variety of exercises at different speeds and always encouraged fast footwork. Following the poles/ cones and ladders the team stretched a second time.

Game One

The team is organized into a 9 v 9 situation (as shown in diagram 114) played in the area between the 18-yard line and the half-line with either small goals or cones. Balls are lined up on the sides of the field to keep the game flowing.

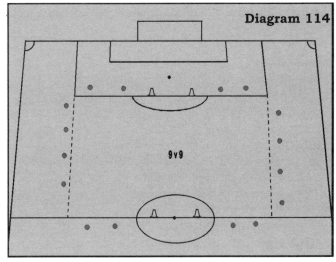

General Points

Players are limited to two-touch with a one-touch finish. Throw-ins are played as normal and the coach keeps the score. Different conditions such as 10 passes equalled a goal, or a goal counts as double, or five goals wins the game are introduced at various stages throughout the session.

Progression

Now play is 8 v 8 in the same area with goalkeepers and full-size goals as shown in diagram 115. Unlimited touches are allowed, with normal throw-ins played. However, if one team wins three corners, they are given a penalty kick. No corners are taken and a goalkeeper starts with the ball.

Points

The coached stressed to the defenders to keep moving up and condense the play thus denying the opposition any space to play in.

The game lasted approximately 25 minutes and was followed by a warm-down jog and team stretch.

Coaching Young Players

Contributed by Brian Mason, Training Director for the JB Marine Soccer Club, St. Louis, MO. Over the years JB Marine has been one of youth soccer's most successful girls clubs with four National Championships, 20 Region Two Championships and 43 State Championships. The following is a series of small-sided games for players in the 6 - 10-year old age group.

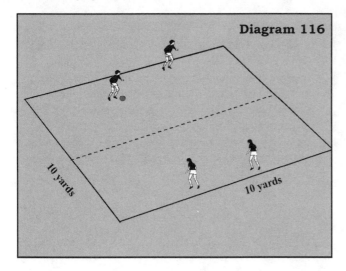

Diagram 116

Shooting Game

Split a small grid in half and play 2 v 2 or 3 v 3 with one team in each half.

Rules

- Players must stay in their half of the grid at all times
- Players try to shoot the ball through the back side of the opposite grid
- Players may use their hands, but if the ball is saved, the player must pass it back with his feet before the next shot can be taken
- The ball must always be moving
- If a team puts a ball out of the side of the grid, the ball goes to the opposition

Grid Goals

Two teams play against each other with a goalkeeper placed in each grid. The objective of the drill is to get the ball to your goalkeeper.

Rules

- Goals are scored if a team plays the ball on the ground to their goalkeeper inside the grid
- The goalkeeper must gather it cleanly
- The goalkeeper is the only player allowed in the grid

Variation

The ball must be passed in the air or headed to score.

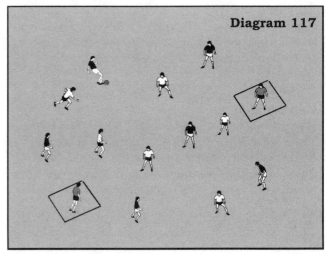

Diagram 117

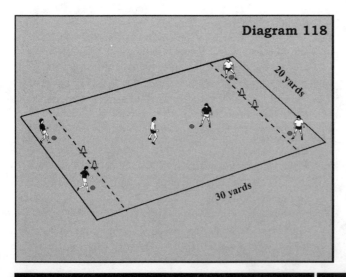

Diagram 118

1 v 1 Transition

Play 1 v 1 in a small area with small coned goals. The rest of the players wait with a ball each.

Rules

- When a goal is scored, a waiting player brings their ball into the area and plays
- The player who scores remains on the field to play the next player

Variation

Play with full sized goals and goalkeepers.

Mick Hennigan

This session on heading, conducted by Mick Hennigan at the WORLD CLASS COACHING International Coaching Seminar, Connecticut, June 2000, was extremely lively, fun and enjoyed immensely by the players. The session is suitable for any level of player.

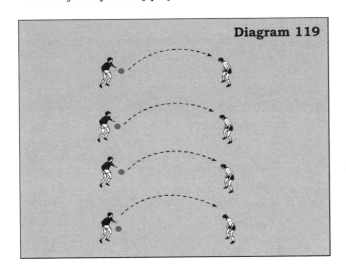

Diagram 119

Warm-Up

Organize the players in pairs, five yards apart. The player with the ball serves to his partner who heads the ball back. Then, instead of serving the ball, the player pulls the ball sharply to his head and heads the ball as hard as possible to his partner.

Warm-Up

This time the server backs up after each time he has served the ball and his partner heads the ball and follows him across the field. Then alternate with the header backing up and the server following.

Juggling

Practice juggling variations such as heading the ball two or three times before heading back to your partner, heading the ball to your partner as high in the air as possible making it difficult for your partner to control with his head, etc.

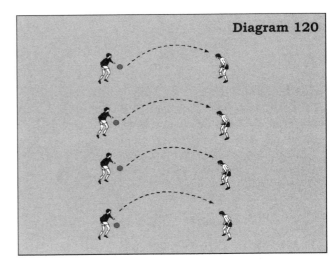

Diagram 120

Diagram 121

Center Circle Game

One team is inside the center circle, the other team is on the perimeter. The team inside juggles the ball only using their heads. Once the ball hits the ground they change places with the perimeter team. Each team keeps count of how many headers they can do.

Coaching Point

Call your name before you head the ball to avoid more than one player attempting to head the ball at the same time.

Mick Hennigan

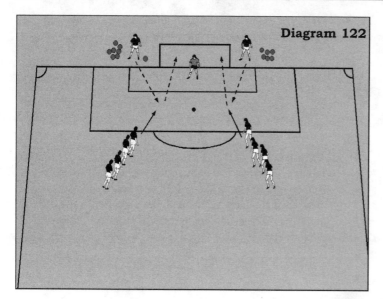

Diagram 122

Heading On Goal

Organize two groups of players outside the penalty area as shown in diagram 122. A server at each goal post serves the ball to the incoming players who try to head for goal past the goalkeeper. The ball must be headed while outside the six-yard box.

Coaching Points

- Head with power - attack the ball
- Head the ball straight, it's easier then a 'glancing' header
- Time your runs - arrive when the ball arrives
- Don't volley - always head it
- Hit the target
- The more heading you do, the more confident you will become

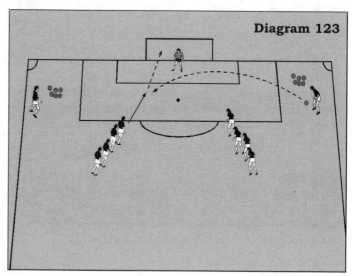

Diagram 123

Heading On Goal

The same organization as in diagram 122, except the servers are now in wide positions. As before, no goals can be scored from inside the six-yard box.

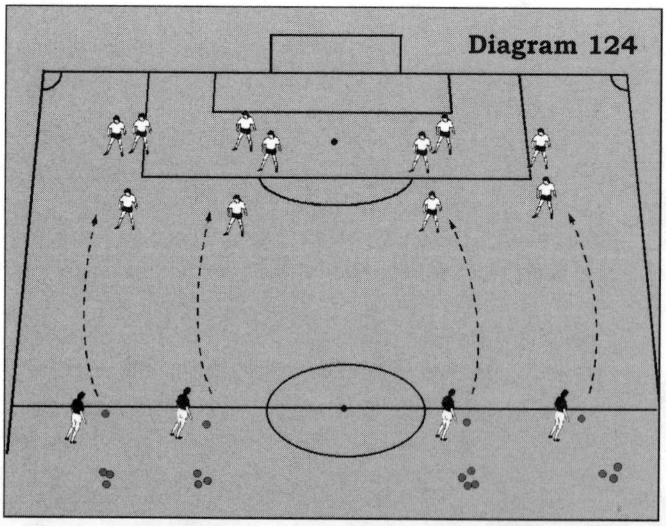

Diagram 124

Defensive Heading

Organize the players in groups on half a field as shown in diagram 124. Each group has a server on the half-line with a supply of balls. The other players in the group line up on the edge of the penalty area. The server plays a firm lofted pass for the player to head away as if he was defending his goal. Then the server passes for the next player in line.

Coaching Point

- Attack the ball
- Head the ball high and far

End practice with a game of throw-head-catch.

PSV Eindhoven - Youth Training

Subscriber Alan Maher has coached at the college and high school level. He has written for the Soccer Journal, Southern Soccer Scene and the New York Times. Alan is also on the board of directors at the NSCAA where he is chairman of printed training material. Alan has been visiting Holland for over 20 years and has watched the training sessions of many Dutch teams. This article is a series of drills executed by PSV Eindhoven youth players. The players are positioned in a 'kite' formation with four players standing as the four points of a kite. The approximate dimensions are 45 x 25 yards but obviously that changes with the players' age and ability. Depending on the number of players available, there will be a few players at each position. Not included is where the players move to after a pass or a run. This differs depending on the drill. Any coach using these drills should be able to experiment and use his/her imagination regarding the rotation of the players.

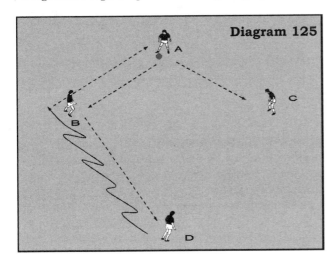

Player A passes to player B.
Player B controls the ball with an open body position and passes to player D.
Player D runs with the ball back to player B's position and passes to player A.
Player A then continues the drill by passing to player C.

Coaching Point

The key to this drill is for player B to control the ball with an open body position to allow him to make the next pass.

Diagram 126 is a progression of the previous drill in diagram 125. This time, the coach positions himself in the middle as shown and player A plays a give-and-go with the coach to start the drill.

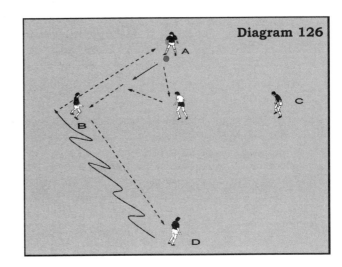

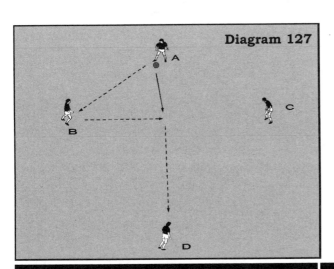

Player A passes to player B.
Player B screens the ball and passes to running player A.
Player A then makes a long-axis pass to player D.

Coaching Points

- Player B must shield the ball and wait for player A to make his run
- Players B and D must move away then check back to the ball to receive it

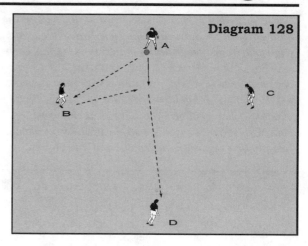

This drill is a progression of the previous drill in diagram 127. This time player B plays a one-touch pass back to player A.

Coaching Point

Player D has to be aware of when player B shields the ball or passes it back one touch so he can time his movement to check to the ball.

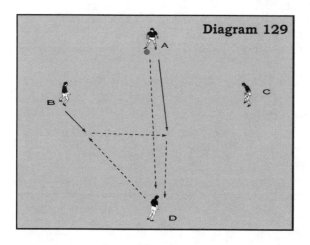

Player A begins with a long-axis pass to player D.
This signals player B to move and support player D.
Player D passes to incoming player B.
Player B passes to running player A.
Player A passes to player D.

Diagram 130 is a quick passing sequence.
Player A passes to player B.
Player B passes a one-touch to player C.
Player C passes a one-touch to running player A.
Player A passes a one-touch to player D.

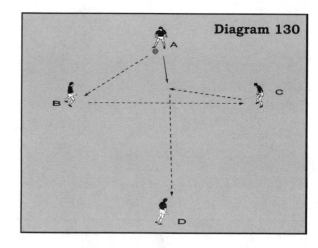

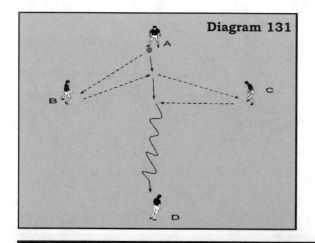

Diagram 131 is a sequence of several quick, one-touch passes.
Player A passes to player B.
Player B passes back to player A.
Player A passes to player C.
Player C passes back to player A.
Player A then dribbles the ball to player D.

OTHER BOOKS IN THIS SERIES

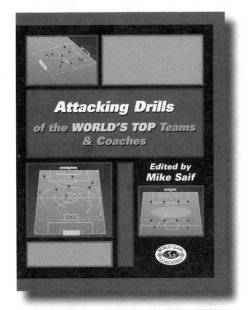

Attacking Drills of the World's Top Teams and Coaches includes training sessions and drills from **Manchester United, U.S. Women's World Cup Team, Venice of Serie "A", Liverpool F.C., Bodens BK of Sweden, Brazilian Youth Teams** plus many of the MLS Teams and other top teams and coaches from around the world.

Over 30 training sessions are included, each with detailed explanations accompanied with easy-to-read diagrams.

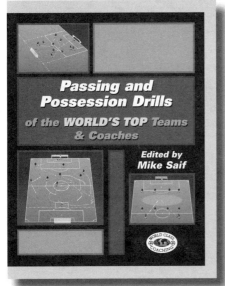

Passing and Possession Drills of the World's Top Teams and Coaches includes training sessions and drills from **Manchester United, Juventus F.C. and Venice of Serie "A", Ajax F.C., Lausanne of Switzerland, Liverpool Academy** plus many of the MLS Teams and other top teams and coaches from around the world.

Twenty-nine training sessions are included, each with detailed explanations accompanied with easy-to-read diagrams.

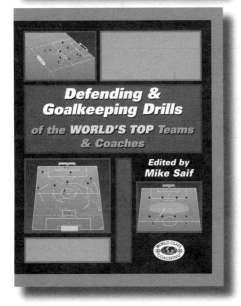

Defending and Goalkeeping Drills of the World's Top Teams and Coaches includes training sessions and drills from **Sao Paulo of Brazil, Italy U15 National Team, Tony DiCicco, Liverpool F.C., Lira Lulea BK of Sweden, Leeds United** plus **New England Revolution of the MLS** and other top teams and coaches from around the world.

Over 20 training sessions are included, each with detailed explanations accompanied with easy-to-read diagrams.

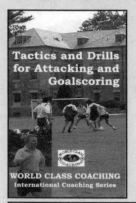
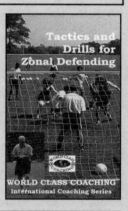